A JUNGLE IN THE HOUSE

By the Author

A JUNGLE IN THE HOUSE

GLUTTONS AND LIBERTINES

THE LAND AND WILDLIFE OF SOUTH AMERICA
    (with the editors of LIFE)

ANIMAL WORLDS

MAN IN NATURE

THE FOREST AND THE SEA

CORAL ISLAND
    (with Donald P. Abbott)

THE DARWIN READER
    (ed. with P. S. Humphrey)

THE PREVALENCE OF PEOPLE

WHERE WINTER NEVER COMES

THE NATURE OF NATURAL HISTORY

THE NATURAL HISTORY OF MOSQUITOES

A Jungle in the House

Essays in Natural
and Unnatural History

MARSTON BATES

WALKER AND COMPANY
New York

To Jake Page and Alfred Meyer

who had the idea

FOREWORD

IN THE FALL OF 1966 JAKE PAGE AND ALFRED
Meyer of *Natural History* magazine came out to see me to
discuss the possibility of my writing a monthly column
for the magazine. We agreed to try it; and since the arrangement was that I would write about whatever happened to
be of concern to me at the time, we decided to call the
column "A Naturalist at Large." The late Thomas Barbour,
for many years director of Harvard's Museum of Comparative Zoology, used this title for an autobiographical book
published in 1943. Tom Barbour was a large man, with
large ideas, who had traveled largely. His travels were on
his mind when he chose the title, and I have always envied
it. There is no copyright on titles, but it would be confusing
to use it for another book and hardly fair to a man whom
I admired greatly and who was in part responsible for
steering me into a career in science — in natural history.

"Natural history." What a grand and proud label! Turning to *Webster's Third New International Dictionary* I
find: "A former branch of knowledge embracing the study,
description and classification of natural objects." "Former"
indeed! When I really want to find out about a word, I
depend chiefly on that stately row of volumes, *The Oxford
English Dictionary* — affectionately known to scholars as
the "OED." Pulling down Volume VII (*N–Poy*), I am

comforted: "A work dealing with the properties of natural objects, plants or animals; a scientific account *of* any subject written on similar lines." (Why is *of* italicized?)

A naturalist is a student of natural history: perfectly simple. But the word has such a great history that it took me a long time to gain the courage to use it. It has characterized such people as Charles Darwin, Thomas Huxley, Alfred Russel Wallace, Henry Walter Bates (no relation). Yet, after all, to be a naturalist doesn't mean you have to be a great one; and for some years now whenever I have encountered a form on which you have to fill in something for "occupation" or "profession," I have written "naturalist" with no qualms. (Where there is a blank for "race" I have always been tempted to write in "human," but I don't remember that I have ever carried through.)

Ours is an age of specialization — necessarily so. But the proliferation of narrow specialties has disadvantages, especially when the labels act as fixed restrictions on the scientists involved. Ecology, ethology, entomology (to pick three "e"s) are important subjects — especially ecology these days; but environment, behavior and insects can all be studied in equal depth under some such general label as natural science. And since we tend to become victims of the labels we use, interrelationships may be more easily seen if we do not think of ourselves as narrowly specialized. In the world of today, with the multiplying problems of man's relations with the rest of nature, a broader point of view becomes increasingly important.

This book is based on the material used for two years

in that *Natural History* column. The order of topics has been changed in the hope of arriving at a more logical sequence, and I have made some additions and deletions. Mostly I have been concerned with the natural history of man, of the human ecosystem: with man's relations with other animals, with his effect on the environment and with the biological background of his behavior. But for the last several years I have found distraction from human problems with the animals and plants in my greenhouse, my "experimental rain forest," and the first several chapters are concerned with this. Why not, then, call the book *A Jungle in the House*? It is far from an adequate label for all of the contents — but the subtitle, *Essays in Natural and Unnatural History*, will hopefully provide a fuller explanation.

CONTENTS

GETTING THROUGH WINTER

1

I AM WRITING THIS IN JANUARY — A NEW year, but also midwinter, with February and March yet to come. The ancient Romans began the year with March, which seems more sensible because the weather was bound to start improving.

Of course I am a victim of prejudice. I was brought up in southern Florida and my first job out of college was with the United Fruit Company in Honduras and Guatemala. Since then I have spent much of my life in the tropics — and always loved it. We lived for eight years in a little Colombian town named Villavicencio in the headwaters of the Orinoco River. *East of the Andes and West of Nowhere* was the title my wife used for a book she wrote about our experiences. We were four degrees north of the equator and visitors used to ask us if we didn't miss the changing seasons — we didn't miss them a bit. But problems like schooling for the children eventually led us to move north to a university town, where their daddy became a professor (though I still have a tendency to flinch when people call me by that title). I reserve the right, however, to grouse about the cold, and about the nasty white stuff that covers the ground for so much of the year.

There is no denying the fascination of winter from the point of view of natural history. Animals, plants — and people — all face the problem of getting through winter, of finding some way of surviving in the unfavorable cold and of coping with the blanket of snow. The curious thing is that from the point of view of geological history this seems to be a relatively new sort of problem. Given the tilt of the planet's axis and the nature of the orbit around the sun, the present zonation of climates seems understandable, even inevitable. Yet the geological evidence all indicates that through most of its history the earth has had a "genial" climate, even at high latitudes, with less marked seasonal changes than those we know.

There is no generally accepted explanation for the climatic changes of the geological past — perhaps no simple explanation is possible. There is evidence that the magnetic poles have not always had their present position; if the north pole were in the north Pacific and the south pole in the south Atlantic, ocean currents could well prevent the polar accumulation of year-round ice. With the poles in their present position — one over the enclosed Arctic Ocean and the other over the Antarctic continent — the dispersal of winter cold is limited and ice accumulates both in the north and south.

During much of the long period when modern forms of life were evolving, permanent ice may not have been present on our planet, unless on high mountains. The fossil vegetation shows that most of the area covered by the United States had a tropical or subtropical climate. To the north the region now covered by the coniferous forests of the taiga shows a temperate flora, comparable with that of the eastern United States now; and Antarctica was covered with similar forests.

Then came the Pleistocene — the Ice Age — with repeated glacial advances and retreats, and with great seasonal fluctuations in climate, at least in high latitudes. What caused this? There is no evidence for polar shifts during this period, though there may well have been changes in the circulation patterns of the oceans and atmosphere. Were the glaciations due to changes in the intensity of radiation received from the sun? Or to changes in the carbon dioxide content of the atmosphere? Carbon dioxide has a "greenhouse effect," warming the earth's surface by reducing heat loss through radiation outward, back into space.

Whatever the cause, the effect is clear: repeated massive accumulations of glacial ice. Geologists are apt to designate the time in which we live as "Recent," dating this from the beginning of the retreat of the last glaciation. But if one looks at Greenland or Antarctica, or if one lives in Michigan in January, it seems to me obvious enough that the Pleistocene is still with us — which makes for problems.

Most birds solve the winter problem by migrating to some region with a more sensible climate, as do people who can afford to live a double life. With the birds the need to migrate seems to be due more to lack of food than to unfavorable temperature in itself. Quite a few birds do manage to stick through the winter if their food habits allow it. Owls continue to harry the local rodents all year round; crossbills live by their expert dissection of pine cones; grouse by eating things like spruce buds. But birds that live on insects and berries have a hard time: not only is the food scarce and difficult to find, but the daylight hours available for searching become limited.

At times I have wondered why migrating birds bother to come north in the spring, why they don't just stay in the more congenial tropics. The answer, of course, lies in the food supply: they can take advantage of the rich possibilities of the northern summer for raising their broods. But how did these often complex patterns of movement get started? What determines which species will migrate and which be homebodies? And why don't some individuals remain instead of facing the long trek home? The migrating instinct has been broken in the opposite direction: a considerable variety of migrants have been known to stay through the winter, supported by bird-loving humans and their feeding stations with seeds and suet. Maybe tropical bird-lovers have not been so obliging with feeders for the summer season.

Long-distance migration depends on flight, which means that mammals (except bats) must find other solutions to the problems of winter. To be sure, a number of mammals change habitats with the seasons: caribou migrating from the tundra into the wooded taiga, where they can dig for fodder in the softer snow; and mountain sheep moving to lower slopes. But such movements are hardly comparable with the journeys of birds. In general, mammals must either find some way of carrying on as usual during the winter months (the weasel solution), or store up food reserves (the squirrel solution) or suspend activities — hibernate (the woodchuck solution).

True hibernation in a mammal involves a considerable drop in body temperature and a slowing of all metabolic processes, including respiration and heartbeat. This is the case with woodchucks, hamsters and hedgehogs in their burrows, and with bats congregated in caves. Bears do not hibernate in this sense, though they may hole up and sleep for most of the winter, living on accumulated fat. In the case of polar bears, most males continue active hunting, but pregnant females dig large dens in snowdrifts, where the young are born.

Snow, from the animal point of view, can be a nuisance, by covering up food; or a blessing, providing a snug refuge. Snow is an excellent insulator, and the temperature under a couple of feet of snow rarely drops below 20°F. even though the air above gets down to 50 or 60 degrees below zero. Small mammals like voles and lemmings are active in their runways and nests under the snow, living on roots, vegetation or stored seeds. It is a dark, silent world under the snow, and the animals there are even protected from many of their usual predators. Sometimes, though, they have to construct ventilating shafts because of the accumulating carbon dioxide, and they risk getting picked up by passing owls at the openings of these shafts.

The smaller mammals have to retreat under snow to maintain body temperature. The smaller the animal, the greater the surface area in relation to body mass; since heat is lost through the surface, a mouse simply cannot keep up its body temperature in a very cold environment. Squirrels are about the smallest mammals that can keep active in the open, and the red squirrel of the north retreats beneath the snow when the temperature reaches the neighborhood of 25° below zero Fahrenheit.

Mammals and birds are "warm-blooded" (the elegant word is *homoiothermic*). In other words, they have some means of keeping their body temperature fairly steady despite fluctuations in the world outside. Reptiles, amphibians, fishes, insects are "cold-blooded" (*poikilothermic*). They have a certain amount of control over body temperature by means of behavior: they can warm up by sunning themselves, or cool off by getting into the shade. But it is difficult for cold-blooded animals to keep warm in winter. The chemistry of life depends on water in a liquid state; if the body actually freezes, if ice crystals are formed in the cells, the system breaks down and the animal dies.

Thus in the north cold-blooded animals must either find someplace to pass the winter where temperatures do not reach the freezing point, or develop a special resting stage in which the water content of the protoplasm is greatly reduced so that its freezing point is lower than usual. Fishes and other aquatic animals are able to keep active in water under the ice, which is usually a few degrees above the freezing point; terrestrial animals frequently dig into the soil.

Amphibians and reptiles have not been notably successful in adapting to northern winters. There are, for instance, 130 species of frogs known from tropical Costa Rica, while Michigan, with three times the area, has only twelve species. Two kinds of frogs get as far north as Alaska. There is an equally dramatic drop in the numbers of snakes and lizards as one goes north from the tropics.

Insects have developed a particularly wide variety of ways of getting through winter. They may hibernate as adults, pupae, larvae or eggs. I have no statistics, but I suspect that winter is most commonly passed in the egg stage. Whatever the form of hibernation, there must be some mechanism for starting the quiescent period before killing temperatures arrive, and for avoiding premature resumption of activity because of an unseasonable warm spell during the winter. A common solution of this problem is "diapause" — a periodic suspension of activity more or less independent of external environmental conditions.

My own experience with diapause has been with mosquitoes. It may occur in these insects in the egg, larval or adult stage, depending on the species. The common European vector of malaria, *Anopheles maculipennis*, hibernates as an adult — large numbers can be found in stables and outbuildings (and sometimes in houses) all through the winter, their abdomens distended with fat instead of with eggs. Mosquitoes usually convert blood into eggs; what causes the prehibernating individuals to make fat instead? I could not find any single environmental factor, like light or temperature. If, however, the mosquitoes were kept under conditions in which they tended to stay quiet rather than flying about, they would accumulate fat; if they were stimulated to daily activity, the fat would be absorbed and eggs formed with the next blood meal. I came to the conclusion that the nature of conditions in September in the Balkans, where I was working — somewhat lower temperatures, shortened twilight period, frequent rains — led to inactivity and hence to fat formation well before the rigors of winter set in.

Most mosquitoes spend the winter (or the dry season in the tropics) in the egg stage, hatching with the onset of spring (or of rains). Many studies have been made of the kinds of stimuli that can break the diapause and cause the eggs to hatch. In general the eggs have to dry out, and then be moistened; with some mosquitoes this is enough. With others, the eggs will not hatch if submerged in plain water, but will if placed in an infusion of dead leaves or similar organic matter. In the case of some species, all eggs will hatch if exposed to the right stimulus; in others, only a few of the eggs will hatch at the time of a particular treatment. This reminds me very much of the complex kinds of factors that govern the germination of seeds; and it has, of course, the same effect — to be sure that all individuals will not be killed as a consequence of some climatic accident.

Most groups of animals and plants show a much greater diversity of species in the tropics than in high latitudes. There has been much speculation as to the cause of this. If strong seasonal changes date only from the beginning of the Pleistocene, a couple of million years ago, maybe there has not been time for evolution to develop winter adaptations in more species. But I suspect that no matter how much time we had for evolution, life would not be as varied in the Temperate Zone or in the far north as in the tropics: conditions, with strongly contrasting seasons, are simply not as favorable as they are with the continuous warmth of the tropics. But this idea may only reflect my prejudice.

Why do we continue to call it the Temperate Zone? It hardly seems an appropriate label for a region where a man may suffer from heat prostration in August and frostbite in February. We have replaced "Frigid" with "Arctic" and "Torrid" with "Tropic." I think something ought to be done about "Temperate."

It began with the Greeks, of course. Pythagoras developed a theory of the spherical earth about 500 B.C.; Aristarchus, about 300 B.C., described the organization of the solar system for which we usually give Copernicus first credit. Eratosthenes in Alexandria, less than a hundred years later, applied these astronomical relationships to earthly map-making. He divided the spherical earth into the five zones that we still recognize, bounded by the lines of the Arctic and Antarctic circles and the two tropics. He called the zones *climata* from the Greek word for incline, referring to the slope of the earth's surface.

The Greeks, of course, were best acquainted with the eastern Mediterranean. They had heard about the frozen seas beyond Thule and they knew about the cold winters of central Europe. But quite logically they were not interested in visiting such barbarous places.

The eastern Mediterranean has a mild climate that might well be called temperate. The Arctic is also, for much of the year, quite appropriately called frigid. As for torrid: the ancients knew the Tropic of Cancer where it crosses the Nile at Aswan, famous now because of Nasser and his dam. "Torrid," according to my memory, is a good description of Aswan, at least in midsummer when I was there. With such conditions at the margin of the tropics, it is no wonder that the ancients thought that life farther south might well be impossible because of the heat.

Our knowledge of the earth has widened since the days of Eratosthenes. "Temperate" may be all right for the eastern Mediterranean, but it hardly seems appropriate for New York, Ann Arbor or Moscow. When you think about it, though, the vocabulary problem is easily enough solved: all that is needed is the prefix "in-."

The Intemperate Zone — that's the way I feel about it in January. It is enough to drive one to drink, to being intemperate in another sense. Even the automobiles need alcohol. There are, of course, people who like winter — the skiers with snow and the skaters with ice; and naturalists have a fine chance to photograph animal tracks in the snow. But I would rather chase butterflies, and my opportunities for that are limited.

But I solved the problem of living through the winter in Ann Arbor a few years ago by bringing a bit of the tropics to Michigan, by building an "experimental rain forest." You can sit out there in January under a hibiscus bush and look at the nasty white stuff outside, while hummingbirds buzz around your ears.

A JUNGLE IN THE HOUSE

2

WHEN PEOPLE ARE COMING TO VISIT US for the first time, we point out that the house is easily identified because of the red front door and the greenhouse on the side. The door is easily explained. It is the consequence of the actions of a guest, a professor from Stanford University, who had a long-suppressed desire to paint something red — and the door seemed a likely object. The greenhouse is another story.

For years we talked about doing something with the screened porch on the southeast corner of the house. We sometimes used it in the summer, but even then we usually preferred to sit outside in the yard. During most of the year it simply accumulated garden furniture and dust. Finally, in the fall of 1964, with winter not far ahead, we were moved to action. We got hold of a contractor who did a most elegant job of converting the porch into a conservatory. The screens were replaced with thermopane

12

windows, the old wooden floor was covered with green tile, fluorescent lights were installed on the ceiling and screened with what I believe is called "eggshell" grill. We arranged a laboratory-like sink in one corner with hot and cold water (it was actually the kind of sink made for use in bars), and put in an electric radiator for heating.

It was November before everything was in order and we could start to look for plants. I ordered a collection of things from a Florida nursery, but they arrived during a cold spell — all dead. So we started with the conventional sorts of plants that were handled by the local florists. But we did find that near Detroit we had one of the best orchid nurseries in the country, where we were able to get a nice collection of unusual species.

Winter set in, and I took to spending an increasing amount of time in my "garden," greatly to the surprise of everyone since I had previously shown no interest in cultivated plants, even when living in the tropics. But the place seemed static — it needed animals.

A friend, returning from Mexico, brought me some small lizards which we turned loose, feeding them fruit flies and mealworms. Another friend gave me a pair of small iguanas for Christmas — promptly named Abélard and Héloïse. Iguanas are vegetarians, so there was no problem in feeding them; though we soon learned that iguanas are incompatible with some kinds of plants — poinsettias, for instance. The garden was presently reduced to the kinds of plants iguanas didn't like to eat: fortunately, this still left a great variety of things. We fed the iguanas lettuce, cabbage, bananas and the like from the market. In nature, iguanas are known to scavenge and we found that ours liked canned dog food.

But why not some birds? I thought about finches as being small, easily maintained and unlikely to do much damage to plants. I did nothing about this, however, until I happened to be in New York later in the winter and got a list of animal dealers from friends at the zoo.

My first visit was to a shop specializing in rare birds — and the owner suggested that hummingbirds would do nicely in my "garden." I hadn't known you could buy hummingbirds: but it confirmed my suspicion that you can get anything in New York if you know where to look (though the shop has since gone out of business, and I know of no dealer there now who handles hummingbirds). I realized that hummingbirds could be maintained in captivity without too much trouble, since a graduate student at the University of Michigan had written his thesis on hummingbird physiology, and had kept his birds in a laboratory across the hall from my office. So I came home with a pair of Gould's violet-eared hummingbirds (*Colibri coruscans*) from the upper Amazon and a pair of honey-creepers (*Cyanerpes caeruleus*) from Costa Rica — as well as a pair of cottontop marmosets and assorted lizards and frogs. The household has not been the same since.

That glassed-in room with the hummingbirds and honey-creepers was marvelous fun — but obviously too limited a space. As soon as weather permitted construction, we added thirty feet of greenhouse along the side of the house.

Lots more plants, lots more birds — a bit of the tropics in Ann Arbor. I had my "experimental rain forest." The problem became how to keep out of it and get anything else done.

We have made many mistakes and — I hope — learned something about the management of plants and animals. In the beginning I really thought I could have a little sample of rain forest, with monkeys, birds, lizards, frogs and various insects happily mixed together in the trees. But this didn't work. Monkeys catch birds and wreck plants simply by climbing over them; birds are quite unpredictable as to what they are likely to tear up in search of nesting materials; small lizards make fine monkey food and also manage to escape by squeezing through narrow openings — and so on.

Soon after the greenhouse was built, I came across a pair of cockatiels in a local pet shop and thought they would look well in the garden. I suppose they had spent most of their lives in a cage — certainly they were reluctant to leave and I had to dismantle the cage to get them out when I took them into the greenhouse. At first they were very shy and spent all of their time up on ladders that I had hung from the greenhouse ceiling. They raised a family in a nest box I arranged up there and gradually gained confidence that the greenhouse was theirs — and started to tear up plants. I didn't want to keep them in a small cage, so I gave them away. Since then I have followed the rule of having no member of the parrot order, no matter how small, attractive and innocent-looking.

When people want to give me presents, they are apt to think that birds would be appropriate — and to get the kinds of birds that are found in pet shops. In this way I have acquired Java sparrows, zebra finches, nun finches and cutthroat finches, which have lived happily in the garden for years without causing any trouble — though zebra finches are incompatible with Spanish moss, which they regard as fine nesting material. I should think such birds would add to the attractiveness of any greenhouse.

Among the gifts were a pair of beautiful weaverbirds (I don't know what species). They seemed to fit in all right, but I soon found that they were stripping leaves, especially of lilies, cannas and banana-like plants, weaving the strips around the wires that held up hanging plants. They never did achieve anything resembling a nest, but they did a good job of tattering many kinds of plants. I decided they had to go. But how to catch two small birds in that mass of foliage? I remembered being at the Lincoln Park Zoo in Chicago one time when a bird got out of its cage in the bird house. The keepers retrieved it by using a hose to get the bird thoroughly soaked so that it could not fly, but could be caught and dried out without damage. A friend and I decided to try this as our only hope. We got the birds all right, but it took about an hour — and we got all of the other birds, and ourselves, thoroughly soaked as well. It is not easy to aim a hose at a small bird dashing about among the bushes, but I still haven't thought of a practical alternative. Those cockatiels that I mentioned before were large enough and awkward enough to be caught with a net, and besides the foliage in the jungle was not so lush then.

The experimental rain forest is divided into three compartments. The original porch is called the Orchid Room, though most of the orchids have been moved out, to be replaced by a variety of shade-tolerant plants, along with hummingbirds, honeycreepers, lizards and tree frogs. Ten feet of the greenhouse proper is partitioned off to form the Monkey Room, where the marmosets live with plants they cannot injure, and the iguanas with plants they will not eat. The remaining twenty feet of the greenhouse forms the Mango Room, named for a flourishing tree from which I hope presently to gather some of my favorite fruit. The fauna there consists mostly of small birds: finches, tanagers and of course hummingbirds. There are also two species of tree frogs which are rarely seen, but make quite a racket at night. The problem is to resist temptation and not get the place overcrowded.

The monkey population now consists of two female cottontop marmosets (*Saguinus oedipus*) named Margaret and Dorothy. For a while I had three squirrel monkeys *(Saimiri sciureus)*. Saimiris are about the gentlest of the South American monkeys, and I had hoped to keep them under more or less "natural" conditions to study their behavior. But they proved to be far too damaging: they would tear up and break plants, and kill birds and lizards when they could get them. I gave them to the Psychology Department the day after they caught one of my favorite hummingbirds.

Even the small marmosets can be difficult. A humming-bird flew through the door into their room the other day and was half eaten before we discovered it. How they managed to catch it I don't know. We now have hung a beaded curtain between the Monkey Room and the Orchid Room, where most of the hummers are, and we exercise great vigilance to be sure we are not followed when we go through the door.

I try to be discouraging whenever people ask me about keeping monkeys as pets. It seems a shame to keep them cooped in small cages; and they can be extremely mischievous if allowed to run loose. They are highly social. One monkey, kept by itself, is likely to pine away if not given constant attention: two or more animals kept together tend to orient toward one another rather than to their owner, however solicitous he may be. Humane societies and zoos are apt to be flooded with offers of monkeys from disillusioned owners.

Marmosets are quite delicate in captivity. We have had several die, sometimes inexplicably, sometimes after the development of "cage paralysis," which seems to be due to a vitamin deficiency. Dorothy and Margaret are in fine shape now — every day they get hummingbird formula mixed with banana paste, fruit and thirty or more meal-worms each, two or three of the worms well oiled with vitamin D solution. Perhaps there would be less difficulty if we were able to concentrate our attention on the marmosets; but there are so many other things calling for

attention that it is difficult to favor any particular inhabitant of the experimental forest.

The hummingbirds remain my favorites. I now have
seven species, and there is endless fascination in sitting in
the room with them and watching what they do. They are
easy enough to keep except that they require attention
twice daily, since they cannot go without food for any·
length of time. For daytime feeding I use a formula
worked out by Bob Lasiewski: brown sugar, 1 cup; Mel-
lin's Food, 1 tablespoon; Gevral Protein, the same; evap-
orated milk, 2 tablespoons; multiple vitamins, 16 drops;
dicalcium phosphate, 2 capsules; water to make one quart.
The feeding tubes are washed thoroughly in the late after-
noon, and filled with a solution of one part brown sugar
to three parts water for the night.

People often ask me if I feed honey to the hummingbirds. The answer is no. Dr. Augusto Ruschi of Brazil,
who has had more experience than anyone else with hummingbirds in captivity, found that honey is liable to
promote a fungus growth on the tongue that kills the
birds. People who try to attract hummingbirds to their
gardens with honey solutions may thus really be causing
damage.

Walter Scheithauer, a German who has been remarkably
successful in keeping hummingbirds, has written a book
on his experiences, entitled *Hummingbirds*. He recounts his
own experiments with diet, and also gives the feeding
formulas used by a number of zoos that have been successful with these birds. The formulas are remarkably

different, though all include proteins (usually some form of baby food), fats, minerals and vitamins — and the zoos listed by Scheithauer all include a certain amount of honey in the diet! Maybe Dr. Ruschi is wrong, or has encountered a situation peculiar to Brazil. Since the formula I use works very well, I haven't wanted to experiment.

Lasiewski's formula includes all of the basic nutrients, and thus would be good food for almost any animal, and in fact I have used it for such different animals as sick iguanas and sick raccoons. Fruit- and insect-eating birds, like honeycreepers and tanagers, also thrive on this formula and most of such birds in my greenhouse have learned to feed from the hummingbird feeding tubes. These other birds cannot hover, but I have fixed perches under some of the tubes. They must have learned about the use of the tubes from watching the hummingbirds.

Hummingbirds in the wild also eat many small insects; zoos and people with aviaries try to keep them supplied with fruit flies. I remember vividly my first experience with this: I had been growing fruit flies in the Orchid Room for the lizards, and when I first introduced the pair of Gould's violet-eareds, the birds cleaned up the flies so rapidly that the lizards starved to death. I now grow large numbers of flies in all of the rooms in boxes of rotting fruit under the benches. Fruit left over by the tanagers, honeycreepers and manakins goes into the boxes, and the corner grocer gives me fruit that goes bad on him. The flies, of course, get all through the house to some extent, and anyone having wine or a drink with fruit juice is liable to find flies in it. But this seems a minor inconvenience.

It is fun to watch the different species bathe. A sabrewing (*Campylopterus villavencensio*) in the Mango Room has the habit of sitting on a wire under the light, where we can watch him from the dining room as we eat dinner, catching the fruit flies that are attracted there. At intervals he takes off to dive into the clear water of a small fountain, going completely under for an instant, and then flying back to the wire to shake out his feathers. The Rivolis (*Eugenes fulgens*) in the same room prefer to slither down the wet leaves of banana plants under a mist nozzle, or sometimes to fly in and out of the rain-like mist.

In the Orchid Room, where the laboratory sink is, the blue-throats (*Lampornis clemenciae*) like to dodge about under a drizzle from the faucet. I put a flower pot upside down with a sponge on it under the dribble, for their convenience. Brunhilde, a most independent-minded blue-throat (all the birds have personal names), will frequently buzz me while I am working there until I stop and set things up for her bath. The honeycreepers like this arrangement too, and there is often some competition. I fixed a small fountain in the room with one of those circulating electric pumps, which seemed to me a perfect place for bathing. The birds tried it sometimes, but they clearly preferred the sink. They have no esthetic sense at all — preferring electric wires to branches, and sinks to fountains.

HUMMINGBIRDS – AND OTHERS

3

THE DOOR FROM THE LIVING ROOM INTO
the experimental rain forest has one of those Chinese
beaded curtains hanging behind it, to prevent birds from
flying through into the house when the door is opened.
I got the idea from the walk-through hummingbird ex-
hibit at the San Diego Zoo; the birds are presumed to fear
entangling their wings in the strings of beads. Actually,
the birds never pay any attention to that door — there is
nothing in the house to attract them — but I feel better with
the curtain barrier.

When I take visitors into the garden, the first thing
that is likely to happen is a thorough inspection of the
strangers by Brunhilde, the female blue-throated hummingbird. She has a habit of hovering directly in front of
their eyes, which can be frightening for people without
eyeglasses. We have thought of keeping a pair of plain
spectacles to lend to such people, though she has never

gone so far as to try probing an eye. If the visitor is a woman with a brightly variegated dress, the colored spots are likely to be investigated; and Brunhilde is usually interested in a ring if it has a brilliant stone. In the case of a man with a sweater, she sometimes tugs at fibers, as though testing possible nesting materials, though I have never seen her make any effort at building a nest, and have never been able to figure out what type of sweater is most likely to arouse her interest.

Each individual bird has a personal name, because each has a distinctive personality — a fact often stressed in the writings of the ethologists Niko Tinbergen and Konrad Lorenz, and often ignored by psychologists studying the comparative behavior of different species of animals. In writing about my birds, I almost inevitably sound anthropomorphic — which is a sin. I have also been accused of teleology, though I am never quite sure what that means, and I don't know whether it is a sin, a misdemeanor or a major crime. But it is clearly reprehensible. Neither of these vices bothers me much, though I have been puzzled by some human attitudes toward animals. The problem of cruelty, for instance — the classic case of ladies in mink coats worrying about the treatment of white mice in the laboratory. (Does anyone worry about chickens in those modern factory-like establishments?)

I think my most unsuccessful lecture to date was one given before the New York Academy of Medicine a few years ago. My topic was the ecology of health, and in the course of the lecture I proposed the formation of a "Society for the Prevention of Cruelty to Parasites." They didn't think it was a bit funny — but don't parasites also have rights? I think the only logical position is that of the Jains of India, who try not to harm any living creature. In our culture I often fail to understand the reasoning behind the decision as to which animals are to be nurtured, and which persecuted — the whole problem of the classification of varmints and pests.

But to get back to anthropomorphism — the widespread disapproval of it by scientists often puzzles me. The person who gets upset by a phrase like "angry bees" will calmly write about a "field of knowledge." Language is built of metaphors, but apparently they are only safe when quite dead through long usage, or in no way open to possible misinterpretation. I think, though, that Joseph Wood Krutch made a good point when he proposed in his book *The Great Chain of Life* that there was an equally dangerous sin in "mechanomorphism" (regarding the animal as a machine). The latter sin is compounded by a resulting awkwardness in writing, but this seems rarely to bother scientists. To be scientific in writing about Brunhilde, for instance, I should have noted that "a particular female of *Lampornis clemenciae* was observed to have a tendency to orient toward spots of brightly contrasting colors." Dull, but perfectly safe.

For me, the most dangerous sin of all in reporting on animal behavior — and perhaps the most common and insidious — is one that doesn't even have a name. It is the sin of thinking that some other kind of animal lives

in the same sensory world that we do. I suppose it could
be called a form of anthropocentrism — another aspect of
our tendency to stay in a man-centered universe. I spent
many years studying the behavior of mosquitoes, and I dedicated the book that came out of this (*The Natural History
of Mosquitoes*) to my first chief, the late Lewis Wendell
Hackett, "able exponent of the importance of trying to
see the world from the point of view of the mosquito." I
never did have much success at this: the sensory world of
the mosquito is so different from mine that I could rarely
be sure what factors initiated or controlled a particular
pattern of behavior. As far as I know we still don't understand what leads a mosquito to bite a particular animal:
or how we are affecting this when we prevent the biting
by smearing repellents on our skins.

With birds and mammals, the situation would seem
to be easier because their sensory systems are for the most
part related to our own. It is still not easy, however. The
problem can be visualized by thinking of what happens
when you go for a walk with a dog. Obviously man and
dog are in quite different worlds — or, as I like to say,
perceptual environments. Those fascinating smells all
around don't mean a thing to a man. The dog's hearing
goes into a higher range than ours, so he picks up many
sounds that we miss. On the other hand, we have much
better eyesight, including color vision, which the dog lacks
— I suppose his environment is all seen in shades of grey.
How could we imagine the effect of colors and the ways in
which they influence behavior if we didn't have color

vision? We have discovered quite a few sense systems that we cannot perceive directly, like the echolocation of bats, and the magnetic fields produced by some fish which enable them to navigate in muddy water by detecting distortions in the field. I suspect that other puzzling aspects of animal behavior may involve sense reactions that we haven't discovered yet.

Thus I have little feeling that I can get the hummingbird point of view toward the little world of my garden. The problem is stated nicely near the end of a book by Stuart Smith and Eric Hosking, *Birds Fighting*. "The really difficult part," they write, "is the interpretation of results once they have been obtained. How can one get behind the bird's eye and learn what is dictating the course of action observed? . . . For the world of a bird, though externally it may be the same world as that in which we live, may appear to that bird a vastly different place from ours." I suppose I would have made this stronger by writing that the bird's world and ours are not even the same place.

With the greenhouse, I think I have stumbled onto a technique that may be useful in many sorts of behavioral studies — something intermediate between caged laboratory experimentation and field observation. My animals are tropical species about whose habits in the wild little is known, but in the few cases where I can make comparisons behavior in the greenhouse seems remarkably similar to behavior observed in the wild. The blue honeycreepers (*Cyanerpes cyaneus*) make a good case, because their behavior in the coffee plantations of Costa Rica has been carefully described in a book by Alexander Skutch, *Life Histories of Central American Birds* — my birds seem to act just like the wild ones.

At the time I am writing, there are representatives of seven families of tropical birds in the experimental area (which covers about 500 square feet): hummingbirds (Trochilidae), honeycreepers and tanagers (Thraupidae); finches (Estrilidae), manakins (Pipridae), sunbirds (Nectariniidae) and white-eyes (Zosteropidae). The white-eyes are the most unusual. Their family includes some eighty-five species of small greenish birds that live almost everywhere in the forests of the Old World tropics, but my particular birds belong to a species (*Zosterops borbonica*) found only on La Réunion Island in the Indian Ocean — I doubt whether there are any others in captivity. A graduate student here spent almost a year on La Réunion studying the habits of the species for his thesis; he brought a number of the birds back with him, and when he had finished his work, gave me the three surviving individuals. Zoology graduate students are extremely helpful in getting unusual animals.

The white-eyes are rather plain-looking, but they are very charming. In nature they live gregariously in large flocks, and my three birds are constantly together, cheeping conversationally as they move about the room, exploring everything. They are primarily insectivorous, and I give them fruit flies and mealworms — but they also readily learned to take hummingbird formula from feeding tubes with nearby perches (as do the quite unrelated honeycreepers); and I suspect this is their chief sustenance, since they pay little attention to the fruit available in their room. They probably learned this through imitation of the honeycreepers and hummingbirds. That birds learn by imitation is proved by the famous case of the British titmice and milk bottles. Back about 1921 some bright British titmouse learned to get cream by opening the cap of the milk bottle. Other birds soon learned, too; in a few years some eleven species had acquired the habit, and it had spread from southern England to the continent — to the distress of the milk companies.

We hope that the three white-eyes include one male and two females, though the sexes are hard to distinguish: it would be great fun to have them breed. So far I have had no success in breeding, except for the too-fertile cockatiels. The female purple honeycreeper, Ethel, keeps trying but something always happens — and we are beginning to suspect that her husband, Bill, isn't living up to his duties. Zebra finches are supposedly easy to breed, and pairs I have had have certainly tried, but in each case the nest has got destroyed through some accident. I have tried to get pairs of birds, but in several cases one has died, and when rare and unusual birds are involved it is far from simple to get another specimen of the proper species and sex.

I have made a special effort to observe aggressive behavior in the garden, since reading that well-known book by Konrad Lorenz, *On Aggression*. The fact that I have only one or two specimens of each species (except for the social white-eyes) makes this difficult, because "aggression" as defined by Lorenz involves fighting among individuals of the same species. So far I have preferred to have a variety of birds rather than a number of the same kind.

Hummingbirds, however, give plenty of opportunity to watch fights. There are seven species in the system and they have been living together for four or five years (none has been added since 1965), yet they seem to have learned little tolerance for each other. I have been trying to think of the appropriate adjective for these birds: aggressive may do, but nasty-tempered, belligerent, quarrelsome seem equally apt.

It would be difficult to prove that hummingbirds are the most belligerent of animals, but they would certainly rank high on any list. I have sometimes thought that they could afford to be nasty because they were so beautiful (there is a scientific generalization for you!). More likely they have been able to develop relative fearlessness because of their mastery of the air. Other birds can fly faster; the Brazilian expert, Dr. Augusto Ruschi, estimates the average speed of hummingbird flight at between five and thirty miles per hour, with thirty as about the maximum. Predatory birds might be able to catch up with them, but no bird could match the aerial acrobatics of hummers, which I imagine enable them to escape easily, at least in the daytime. And they are so agile that they can get involved in very vicious-looking fights among themselves without real damage. I am somewhat puzzled as to how monkeys have managed to catch hummingbirds in my greenhouse: perhaps a consequence of confinement and the fact that the birds have become fearless.

Unfortunately most of the 319 known species of hummingbirds live in remote tropical American forests, while most students of animal behavior live in Europe or North America. Only one species, the ruby-throat, reaches the eastern United States; eleven species have been found to breed in the western part of the country, but some of them only close to the Mexican border — these figures from Crawford Greenewalt's beautiful book, *Hummingbirds*.

All observers agree about the belligerence of hummingbirds; but they do not fit Lorenz's concept of intraspecific aggression, because every individual seems to be at odds with every other at times, regardless of species or sex. Frank Pitelka, the American student of animal ecology and behavior, summarized many of the early descriptions in the issue of *The Condor* for September–October 1942. In his own observations on ruby-throats, he noted that they sometimes chased bees and hawkmoths as well as other ruby-throats (the only kind of hummingbird available). He thought that buzzing flight may have been, at least in part, the stimulus for attack.

In the greenhouse, any new hummingbird causes an uproar, with dreadful-looking fights that make me want to pitch in and separate the antagonists — despite the obvious futility of such action. But I have never been able to detect direct physical injury. As I remarked, the fights continue sporadically, even when the birds have been living together for years. But the interspecies belligerence

seems to be purely among the hummingbirds themselves —
they ignore other birds, even the honeycreepers when they
are using the hummingbird feeders which have perches.
Maybe Pitelka is right, the buzzing sound is required as a
stimulus. Or maybe the aristocratic hummingbirds simply
can't be bothered with the actions of lesser creatures.

Belligerence among animals takes many forms. One is
against possible predators. I have not been able to do
much with this because the only predators in the garden
are small lizards and frogs. But Dr. Ruschi in Brazil
catches his hummingbirds by using a tame owl as a decoy
in the forest: all of the neighboring hummingbirds gang
up to pester the owl, and Dr. Ruschi then catches them
with a fishing pole greased with linseed oil — the wings
are easily cleaned, and the captured bird can be released
in a huge screened cage. (Brazil has advantages over Michigan as a place to keep captive hummers.)

I thought it would be interesting to try the reaction of
my birds to a stuffed owl. If they attacked it, then we
could start making various owl-like models to see whether
we could determine the nature of the "essence of owl" that
sets the hummingbirds off. It turned out, however, that
one of the graduate students had a tame owl, so it seemed
much better to start with this. We took the owl out into
the garden with considerable trepidation — but nothing
happened! The hummingbirds paid no attention, and the
owl simply looked confused. I cannot doubt Dr. Ruschi's
catching method; and some of my birds in this experiment
were Brazilian, so it cannot be a geographical difference.

My only explanation is that my birds had been protected in captivity for so long that they had lost their innate fear reactions — but this upsets my idea about the "naturalness" of observations under the greenhouse conditions. It remains a puzzlement — to be tried again one of these days.

Lorenz's studies on aggression also raise questions of territoriality — of areas defended by individuals, pairs or social groups against intrusion by other members of the same species. Hummingbirds, it turns out, also fail to fit neatly into the various sorts of territorial classifications. My first two birds, Gould's violet-eareds (*Colibri coruscans*), were released in the Orchid Room in 1965. We thought they were a pair, and named them Gamon and Spinach with memories of the nursery rhyme. But the sexes are difficult to distinguish in this species, and when the two birds promptly started to fight, we began to wonder about their sex. After considerable squabbling, they divided the room almost exactly in half with frequent vicious fights at the boundary line. A visiting ornithologist was sure we had two males, but Spinach disproved this by building a slipshod nest in the top of a *Dracaena* plant and laying two eggs — which presently fell through the bottom of the nest to break on the floor.

Hummingbirds are known to build neat and sturdy nests, but they use such materials as spider webs for binding. But spiders don't have a chance in the Orchid Room with the honeycreepers constantly on the alert for such tasty morsels. We have tried various sizes of tea-strainers as bases for nest-building. The honeycreepers take to this, but Spinach has so far scorned such gadgets even when they have been placed at a point where she has started to build a nest. The German amateur ornithologist Walter Scheithauer, in his book *Hummingbirds,* reports success in breeding several species by providing a collection of different possible types of nesting materials, but I suspect he has more persistence and patience than I have; and he may have more amenable species.

Field evidence (summarized by Pitelka) indicates that hummingbirds in the wild are apt to set up a territory-like defense of favored feeding areas — the same thing I have observed with feeding tubes in the greenhouse. Nesting females also defend an area around the nests (male hummingbirds are completely indifferent to family affairs except for the brief period of mating), but all such arrangements are apt to be temporary and shifting. It is interesting that with my birds, only hummers ever pass through doors into strange areas. Even when a door is propped open for some reason, the other birds all stay at home. The greatest wanderer of all is Brunhilde: she particularly likes to get into the Monkey Room, I suppose because it is a fine place to hunt fruit flies since no birds live there. This tendency to wander has led me to hang a Chinese beaded curtain between the Orchid Room and the Monkey Room as well as the one behind the door into the living room.

One of the nice things about being a professor is that there are students around — and I have had several undertake research projects in the garden. One of the first was to test hummingbird color preferences. There is a widespread belief that hummingbirds are attracted to red: the commercial feeders sold for people to hang in their gardens are always marked with red. We arranged a series of feeding tubes in a row and then tagged each with a piece of paper of different color and checked the number of visits to each tube. It turned out that the birds were quite indifferent to the color (except that yellow was slightly less attractive than red, green or blue), but they showed a strong preference for position, visiting most often the tubes at each end of the row. After we had done all of this, we discovered that several other people had done the same thing — and got the same results. Yet, at least in the southwestern United States, flowers depending on hummingbirds for pollination are generally colored red, which seems contradictory.

This problem, with its possible explanation, has been explored by Karen and Verne Grant in a fascinating book entitled *Hummingbirds and Their Flowers*. The Grants point out that "Hummingbirds, in learning to associate red floral colors with availability of large quantities of nectar, would benefit in quickly finding new floral food sources through recognition of their red colors. This ability to find new food sources without going through a trial and error process would be particularly advantageous to migratory hummingbirds which continually enter new feeding territories." If this theory is correct, it is interesting that each bird must learn the meaning of the red signal — while the coloration of the flowers is fixed by evolutionary adaptation. This learned preference for red seems to be easily lost in captivity — though when the Grants tested feeders with different colors on wild birds in their California garden, they again found no clear preference for red. Which is puzzling.

Studies in the garden have taught me a lot, even though we haven't turned up anything very startling or original, and I think it has been good practice for the undergraduates, several of whom have gone on into graduate work in behavior. I think it would be a good idea for every university to have a large greenhouse with both plants and animals, but so far I haven't been able to persuade any to try it. The botanists say that they wouldn't be able to fumigate — but with a few sharp-eyed insect-eating birds around, fumigating is superfluous. Of course, there are hazards from not being able to introduce poisons into the system. With us the major difficulty has been with cockroaches — not in the garden, but migrating out into the house. My wife, Nancy, can tell that story best — I tend to shrug and regard it as her problem.

A HORDE UNCOUNTABLE

4

IN CHAPTER TWO THE BOSS REMARKED THAT with the setting up of the garden, the arrival of hummingbirds and honeycreepers, of Héloïse the iguana and the assorted monkeys, "The household has not been the same since." For a long time, we of the household fully shared his boundless enthusiasm. We reveled in the delight of seeing a red hibiscus flower blooming against the background of midwinter snow, or the joy of feeling a hummingbird's tiny feet on our fingers at feeding time. We did not realize then that we should become less and less the same and with somewhat diminishing pleasure. Because, as a chapter title in the Boss's book *Coral Island* proclaims, there are "Flaws in Paradise."

Anyone playing God in a small way, even in 500 square feet of space, is bound to have failures in establishing balances among flora and fauna. And with these failures, such as the necessary departure of the over-heavy saimiri monkeys and the over-fecund cotton rats, the death for a variety of reasons of birds, lizards and monkeys, the utter disappearance of several finches and a large number of bright little frogs from Colombia, and the truly tragic loss to all of us of Bronzy, tamest and most charming of the hummingbirds, we have been learning by trial and error.

On the other hand, Héloïse has been rescued from what seemed the final stages of starvation by force feeding, the marmosets were rejuvenated by extra vitamin D as suggested in Gerald Durrell's book *Menagerie Manor,* and Ethel the honeycreeper has hatched two eggs — though the nestlings both died within ten days — and is still devotedly brooding her fifth or sixth clutch in the tea-strainer by the door. Successes and failures: we of the household have followed them all with interest and sympathy. WITH ONE EXCEPTION! I refer to the invasion, as the garden has grown, of a host, a horde uncountable, of cockroaches.

Hidden in the soil of plants from Florida or the packing that brought reptiles safely from Colombia, the egg cases of several species must have landed in comfortable places about the garden, there to hatch and start this process. Fine and dandy, if, like the birds, monkeys and Héloïse, they would all remain in the garden to add to the natural fauna of this "experimental rain forest"; but they didn't and they don't. We have long been accustomed to houseflies and fruit flies, but cockroaches are something else again.

In an article in *Harper's* for December 1966, Dr. Howard Evans extols the wonders of "The Intellectual and Emotional World of the Cockroach" and claims that, struc-

turally unchanged since before the advent of man, cockroaches are not only tremendously adaptable but also train-
able. He heartily commends the cockroach, though he says
"He must, of course, be met on his own terms, in his
own world." With his world and mine overlapping more
and more, this phrase has come to have a sinister meaning
for me as time goes on. Dr. Evans maintains they make
fine experimental animals. Could they, I wonder somewhat desperately, be trained to stay in the garden and not
in the kitchen, the basement, even upstairs among our
toothbrushes? Dr. Evans is most welcome to come and
try; we have space to spare and would put him up indef-
initely. Could they be trained to lay their eggs in moist
sand as he saw one species do in a Florida state park, or
don't we have the egg-burying kind? Most probably not,
for there are 3,500 species now in existence (of which
"fewer than 5 per cent have been studied in any detail,"
to quote Dr. Evans again), and our luck has surely brought
us the kind or kinds that never thought of such a thing.

The article, incidentally, is fascinating if somewhat discouraging to the housewife put at bay by the roach's agil-
ity, fertility and ingenuity. In this house they do not simply
drop their egg cases on the floor anyoldwhere, where at
least we might destroy some of them; they hide them under
alarm clocks, behind books, in the dark recesses at the backs
of kitchen drawers, all over the basement, and even somewhere in the living room, judging by the population
explosion there.

Surely it is unnecessary to describe the feelings of a

middle-class, middle-aged, Midwestern housewife when confronted with cockroaches not only in her cupboards but in the teakettle, not only in the breadbox but in the refrigerator! True, my housekeeping is casual and intermittent, guaranteed to make the efficient feel smug and the inefficient feel at ease, perhaps even superior. But in spite of this — the dishwasher full of dirty dishes, unwashed pots and pans waiting either for my high level of tolerance to be exceeded or for the arrival of Maggie who cleans for us — in spite of this, during all the previous years in our house we had encountered only one cockroach. Now the place reminds me of the town of Hamelin before the coming of the Pied Piper.

Symbols as they are of dirt, disease and sloppy housekeeping — though I might add here that the experts find them less unclean than many other types of vermin — roaches are the only creatures I have a real horror of, to which my reactions are instantaneous and violent. Rats, mice, snakes and lizards, spiders, chiggers, mosquitoes, wasps, even lice — which were found on my head at about the age of ten and combatted, somewhat drastically, I thought, with kerosene — almost all creeping things are to me "nature's creatures" just like us. Except cockroaches. But then it seems to me that almost everyone has a horror of something special: some people don't mind roaches but can't stand spiders, some go in deadly fear of wasps or bees. Lizards must be high on the list, so high that it is forbidden by law to sell them in pet shops in Detroit. I used to wonder if anyone had tried to catalogue or categorize the various things that people are afraid of. Well, according to a book entitled *Men and Snakes,* by Ramona and Desmond Morris, a survey of this sort was done in England in April 1961, and repeated in October 1962, using TV and a national newspaper to ask the questions "Which animal do you like most? Which animal do you dislike most? Which animal topic would you most like to see dealt with in future animal programmes on television?" I find it interesting that cockroaches are not on the list of the top ten dislikes at all, but that while snakes topped the list by a vast majority, spiders came second. I now go about asking my friends the first two questions, but in my anecdotal way can report only that reptiles do seem to hold first rank, with snakes more feared than lizards. Even the Boss has often remarked that he is sure if he were bitten by a snake he would die of fright!

This last fact is a comfort to me in fighting what must be an "imprint" in the Lorenzian sense, for how else to explain this terror, this completely automatic revulsion that seizes me when a large roach lands upon me? After all, I was brought up mostly in Florida where all these beasties abound. I also had a big brother who put June bugs down my neck or fluttery moths in my hair as big brothers often do. My reaction to this was to set out to learn not to fear them, to hold them in my hand, to feel the flutter of a moth's wings or the rasp of a June bug's legs. Why then can't I hold a gentle, harmless cockroach? This challenge has gone unmet during many years in Florida and in Colombia, S.A. Will it now come to pass that I shall overcome my weakness in Ann Arbor, Michigan? For surely it is a weakness unworthy of a naturalist's wife.

Just the other day the Boss handed me a book by John Rublowsky entitled *Nature in the City,* with the remark that the chapter on "Crawling Things" might be of interest to me. It was, if perhaps not in the way he intended. It only increased my feeling of being engaged in an endless losing battle against these representatives of "one of the oldest life forms in the world." Our huge old house is an ideal habitat for those who thrive in warm dark places. We can almost hear them munching, not only on our food and that of the pets, but also on our books, on the papers in our files, on soap and wool and even shoe polish. Leave an opened package of cigarettes too long in the same place and the cigarettes are riddled with tiny holes where the paper has been chewed. Leave the dregs of your wine on the living-room table at night and in the morning it will be crowded with the dead and the dying. Anything missing or mislaid is blamed on them these days. Who took Ethel's first nestling from her nest at the age of three days? Who cleans up the turtles' tray each night, when, having only two, we put out enough food for six? Who, indeed, made off last week with $25.00 from my wallet and half a bottle of bourbon?

Mr. Rublowsky says, "Though the mature roach has well-developed wings, it rarely flies, and then only for a short distance." I guess I'm wondering how short he considers this distance to be. Our living room is fairly large, yet they have been seen to fly from the mantelpiece to the couch against the opposite wall, often landing on some unsuspecting visitor. And I remember all too well one midnight in our baby's room in Colombia being set upon by a horde of them — more probably two in truth, but you know how it is. They arrived by air and my whinnying brought the Boss from his bed out of a sound sleep.

Mr. Rublowsky also maintains that the sound of roaches scuttling to safety in the dark may be responsible for certain ghost stories — that they make a "dry and brittle rattling sound." This we have not noted, nor have we, close as they are to us, observed any particularly strong smell about them, despite what he says on that score. But then perhaps since we are smokers all, our noses are not as keen as his.

So far, we seem to have two species in the house, though no doubt there are several more in the garden (remember, 3,500 species in all!) well able to find their way where others have blazed the path. The less objectionable, though more in evidence, being not nearly so coy and nocturnal as the others, are the small, narrow, light-greyish kind — *Blattella germanica* is the scientific name — otherwise known as croton bugs. Much worse are the *Periplaneta americana*; they zoom about like miniature bats, particularly under pursuit by one of us armed with a spray bomb. As stated before, when they land on me, I whinny like a wounded horse. When you step on them they crunch. And what DOES one say as a hostess when a guest, or perhaps one of our seminar students, sitting on the living-room rug, recoils and points and says, "WHAT is that?" My embarrassed and apologetic explanations are variously received, to the obvious glee of the Boss, who sits by, also on the floor of course, and grins. After all, he likes cockroaches. It was interesting, perhaps downright comforting, to have him admit not long ago that even he was somewhat taken aback, on going into the garden at night after the lights had been off for a bit, to find a wall-to-wall carpeting of roaches!

Of far greater comfort, however, is the fact that the other members of the household feel as I do. Marston, devising an ingenious method of trapping roaches alive, was at first all for returning them to the garden. But the rest of us would have none of that; they are either scalded to death and flushed down the drain or squashed and thrown in the garbage. And in the evenings around the kitchen table when we hear the water heater in the basement going "blurp, blurp, blurp," Bruce, who rooms upstairs, will look at me darkly and say, "There they go, at it again. Drilling in formation they are, arming against us." Jerry and Marcos, who live in the basement, keep traps and spray bombs in their rooms to avert being awakened by creepy crawlings in the night. In Jerry's absence, however, my daughter Marian and her husband proved less enduring; the second night, disturbed by strange rustlings and the feel of something crawling over Andy's back, they moved and found an unoccupied bed upstairs. This led to an all-out attack in that room, which revealed not only a great many cockroaches but a number of other oddments such as my mother's antique ivory beads, books from the Boss's library and endless feminine impedimenta left behind by daughters who, while not really like cockroaches, do have a tendency to go off with things and redistribute them unpredictably. We also found, to Maggie's great and audible distress, a tiny baby lizard that proved to be of the same kind that we had in the garden — encouraging proof that the pair we had introduced but never saw were breeding. Geckos just love cockroaches!

The Boss's traps, mentioned above, having proved so effective, perhaps I should describe them. Simply take a laboratory fingerbowl — or any smooth-sided, widemouthed container — and grease the inside walls. Oil, butter, bacon fat, almost anything slippery will do (except vegetable shortening, which seems too solid), and with a bit of pet food, hamburger or almost anything as bait you can attract the monsters in to where they cannot climb out nor yet have room to take off in flight. We have counted as many as thirty caught in one bowl hidden overnight. At first we took great care to hide these traps lest the three cats and two dogs who share the house with us get there before the roaches. But when we began to find roaches drowned in glasses of wine or beer left overnight in the living room it occurred to us that this might be the ideal bait, for the pets, unlike most of the people around here, are non-alcoholic. And then in a bulletin on *The Principal Household Insects of the United States*, written in 1896 by L. O. Howard and C. L. Marlatt, we found a specific recommendation of stale beer as bait. Both authors were close friends of my father; indeed Dr. Marlatt was "Uncle Charles" to me. In the section on remedies Dr. Marlatt gives a number of trap designs, all on the same principle of enticing roaches in to where they cannot get out. Being liberally supplied with lab bowls, roly-poly highball glasses and widemouth jars, we have been running experiments in the garden using various materials as bait, and can now report that beer has it all over red wine, white wine and bourbon and water, even though, as Marston remarked, "It was the very best bourbon." Pet food still runs beer a close second, but a great advantage of beer is that the creatures drown, while with the non-liquids they have to be killed, which is always an unpleasant and somewhat guilt-producing process. Unless, of course, one has aggressions to get rid of.

At this point, our readers are probably wondering why on earth we don't tear the place apart, spray every nook and cranny, every possible hiding place. Well, that's quite a large order in a seven-bedroom house with three floors— no, four if you include the attic, a repository for the belongings of numberless people over numberless years—and with bookshelves crammed to overflowing in nearly every room. Or why not call in an exterminator? Ah, but remember, we have a jungle in the house, or right next to it: a small bit of rain forest, a tiny "ecosystem," a living work of art. It is quite possible that just one cockroach escaping the exterminator might carry the garden's doom on his prickly feet. I remember well, after reading Rachel Carson's *Silent Spring,* how we welcomed the presence of fruit flies in our cups of wine, even were pleased to see houseflies and ants as proof that there was no DDT about. We remember the robin someone brought us, picked up from his lawn, that died in convulsions as we held it. Robins still seem scarce around here the first days of spring; they do not wake us at dawn as they used to. Such dreadful poison would not take long to go from roaches to fruit flies and through them to the hummingbirds. So now when we do spray, it is with great circumspection, using compounds that contain no DDT and not in the rooms adjoining the garden. I must admit, however, that this is a fragile principle, and that in practice, in the heat of the chase, some of us have—and not seldom—pursued an enemy over the forbidden line into the dining room and the living room. It is so easy to forget at such a time.

Some months ago Archie Cowan, Associate Professor of Wildlife Management (wild life indeed?), came by to view the garden and over a few drinks informed us that he had a very fine white silicate powder which had such a desiccating effect that when merely walked over by roaches it dried them up in a matter of minutes. It was also harmless to most other animals. This powder, to be put out by, among others, the Davidson Chemical Company of Baltimore, Maryland, under the name "Dry-die 67," is composed of silica aerogel and ammonium fluorosilicate. His offer of a sample was quickly accepted, and when it arrived we immediately put it to the test. The reaction, while not instantaneous, was quite remarkable. Within a few hours roaches came staggering out from everywhere, a great many, oddly enough, from behind the door-gong on the kitchen wall. And for a while there seemed to be a lessening of the invasion, with dried corpses turning up in the most peculiar places. But the process of sprinkling powder around at stated intervals is a tedious one, demanding more organizational ability and consistency than I am capable of. Besides, you don't get the spectacular results, the visual impact of a whole bowlful of the enemy drowned in stale beer. Blessings on you, Uncle Charles, now dead these many years, for that bulletin written in 1896! For a while I toyed with yet another remedy taken from this same bulletin. It seems that the great freeze of 1894 in Florida, "which was so destructive to the citrus groves, on the authority of Mr. H. G. Hubbard, destroyed all the roaches, even those in houses, except a few unusually well protected." My idea, come midwinter, of sealing off the garden, which has its own heating system, turning off the house furnace and retiring to a motel for a day or so was scotched by the Boss's usual practicality. "What about the water pipes?" he asked (they supply the jungle too).

And so, with spray bombs, the white powder that is not yet on the market, and above all with beer, the battle goes on, and will go on, for we know that in the garden the legions are growing to the point where even Marston's co-operation is no longer in doubt. He is afraid the roaches may eat up all the rotting fruit that breeds the fruit flies that feed the hummingbirds, the frogs and the lizards. There was a time, though, not so far back, when he mentioned several times that a guy over in the Entomology Department at the University's Museum of Zoology had offered him roaches from Madagascar as big as mud turtles, and as he said this, a sort of speculative, almost wistful gleam would come into his eyes.

It is, however, a constantly changing situation, for not only are we finding the *Periplaneta* to be definitely driving out the croton bugs, but we of the household are showing distinct signs of adaptation as well. Now, of an evening when a few come crawling out of the stove at the onset of cooking, provided they are small enough, I can coolly squash them with a finger, saying "Die!" in triumphant tones, and count them as they are dropped into the garbage pail. It has also become easier to step on the large and crunchy kind, possible to look closely at a huge one in a trap, even to touch an antenna before pouring on the boiling water, perfectly easy to pick up the occasional desiccated corpse. But let one land upon me and the old revulsion sets up the immediate and violent reaction. Only the other day, encountering a large *Periplaneta* half drowned in the sink, I determined it was now or never, and with a pair of tweezers picked him up. With a surge of courage I held him tightly between thumb and forefinger; and I looked him in the eye, let his one free feeler wave about in a feeble dying way. Interesting he certainly was, the head so tiny and hidden compared to the rest of him, his brown covering with its curious markings even handsome in a way. But not lovable, not interesting enough to me just yet to escape death. However, as they say in Spanish, *poco a poco se anda lejos* ("little by little one goes a long way"); and who knows, I may yet come to accept these flaws in Paradise casually.

I was about to add here a plea in general for some small, active and preferably nocturnal animal, be it mammal or lizard, that lives largely on cockroaches, when who should turn up but Don Tinkle from the museum with a pair of *Uta palmeri*, medium-sized blue-grey lizards that he claims are exceedingly fond of roaches. One promptly died, but the other we presume to be going about his business. And after Tinkle came Arnold Kluge with some thirty more geckos, which disappeared in a trice when liberated in the Orchid Room. These may be too small to handle the adult *Peris*, but it is a marvelous comfort to go into the garden at night and find a half dozen or so busy with their hunting of the young. Perhaps in time we can achieve a balance there. Meantime it does seem as though the daily haul from the beer traps is declining, with fewer adults of breeding age, so perhaps in the house too a balance may be found. It has been suggested that we might loose geckos in the house. But the price of that would be far too high, for we should immediately lose Maggie, our household helper. Reptiles, all of them, are to her what roaches are to me. Each to his own distaste as it were.

Lest this tirade tend to discourage anyone from building a bit of tropical rain forest in the "Intemperate" Zone, let me insist that the price which we have paid for it is far outweighed by the joy that the jungle in the house has given us. We've grown accustomed to the warmth, the sounds, the smells of the tropics coming to us when winter is outside. Most of the birds, the monkeys and the iguana have personal names—Marston has already written a good deal about

Brunhilde and Héloïse—and Ethel's never-ending maternal urge has us all fascinated. Is this latest clutch fertile as the past three have not been? If she hatches, will they live as the first two nestlings did not? We are just as eager as the Boss is to add the call of tree frogs to the chorus in the garden. And even the "invasion" has provided the excitement of a campaign, a number of pseudoscientific experiments and a great deal of laughter.

HELOISE AND OTHER HERPS

5

So, WE HAVE COCKROACHES. I WISH I HAD kept a precise record of the population explosion. Several months ago, when we first became cockroach-conscious, the large *Periplaneta* and the smaller *Blattella* were about equal in numbers. Now, as Nancy said, the *Periplaneta* are overwhelmingly more numerous. It looks as though they have won in competition, and it would be interesting to have this neatly documented. We know all too little about the nature of competition among species — and here we had a good chance to study it right under our noses.

In introducing possible predators to combat the cockroach proliferation, we have limited ourselves to small lizards and frogs, because of danger to nestling birds — and these animals may not be able to handle the large adult *Periplaneta*. Our only large lizard is an iguana named Héloïse — perfectly safe because iguanas are primarily vegetarian.

Héloïse is also the oldest animal inhabitant of the garden, having been given me, along with Abélard, on Christmas 1964. Abélard arrived with an injury and died within a few days. Héloïse, now that she has grown, turns out to be a male, but we have got too used to the name to change it for such a trivial reason.

We have become quite fond of Héloïse during the years she (he or it) has lived with us. I am not at all sure, however, that this feeling is reciprocated. Héloïse gives the appearance, from her perch high in a bush or on a greenhouse rafter, of looking down on people, disdainfully. It is said that iguanas become quite tame and used to handling; but not Héloïse. I tried picking her up every day for a month, but she never learned to like this, always squirming and scratching vigorously. She does, however, go into a sort of trance when I stroke her around the ears — seemingly in blissful contentment.

Iguana-watching is a very dull occupation, since the lizards remain stretched out for long periods in some comfortable place, rarely moving. They illustrate beautifully the dictum of the British ecologist Charles Elton that "All cold-blooded animals . . . spend an unexpectedly large proportion of their time doing nothing at all, or at any rate, nothing in particular." A graduate student here at the university, Walter Moberly, wrote his thesis on iguana behavior and physiology and spent one summer observing wild iguanas in Colombia — like Héloïse, they moved only rarely, and then only to forage, to seek a better basking place or to escape a possible predator.

Iguanas are most common in forests along streams, and when alarmed they drop either to the ground or into the water — Moberly saw them drop as much as sixty feet, without apparent harm. They can stay under water for considerable periods of time and seem to be good underwater swimmers; this is their favorite method of escape.

The vegetarian habit of iguanas is unusual among lizards. A friend has told me of an iguana he kept for several years that would eat mealworms, but this is the only instance of such a habit that I know of. Héloïse scorns mealworms, but she will eat canned dog food and hard-boiled eggs. Iguanas in the wild have been observed to eat carrion.

I find Héloïse's taste in vegetation quite unpredictable, except that she tends to like plants with a milky sap: poinsettias and papayas, for instance. I have several potted poinsettias which, when they have a good growth of leaves, I move into the room where Héloïse lives as food for her. She also likes things like lettuce, cabbage and collards. A friend gave me some seeds of *Cannabis sativa* (hemp — or, if you will, marijuana) left over from an experiment with the hashish fudge described in *The Alice B. Toklas Cook Book*. The seeds germinated and started a healthy growth, only to be demolished by Héloïse. She seemed, at this time, as imperturbable as ever; if she had a psychedelic experience, there were no visible signs. Héloïse also tends to like flowers, even of plants that she will not otherwise touch, such as water hyacinths or water lilies.

I would especially like to learn more about the amphibia and reptiles — lizards, frogs and turtles — collectively known as "herps" from the science of herpetology. I would dearly love to establish breeding colonies of some of these. At the moment there are ten species of frogs, four of lizards and one species of land turtle (the South American *Geochelone carbonaria*). In many cases there is only one specimen of a given species — so that reproduction is, to say the least, unlikely. Small tropical frogs and lizards are hard to come by from the usual animal dealers because they are not sufficiently spectacular to interest most people, so I have to take whatever I can get, from dealers or from friends.

The small herps are difficult to find even in the confined area of my garden — which makes me understand why their behavior has been so little studied in the wild. Hiding species would be impossible to locate in the rain forest, except for the ordinary collecting method of making their eyes gleam at night with a flashlight.

There is an interesting difference in how my tree frogs spend the daytime. One individual of a rather large grey species, *Hyla septentrionalis,* can almost always be found in the same place for periods of several weeks before it shifts to some new hiding place. For a while this *Hyla* used the hollow in the end of a tree fern trunk; then it hid for several weeks in a bromeliad growing on the same fern trunk; after this it took to a hollow in a brick. At the moment it has some new hiding place that I haven't yet located.

This contrasts strongly with the behavior of a bright green Mexican tree frog, *Phyllomedusa callidryas,* in the same room. I do not see the *Phyllomedusa* for weeks at a time, but whenever I do locate it, it is in a different place, all hunched up on top of a leaf and almost impossible to make out because it blends so perfectly with the foliage.

Biologists recognize territory as an area defended by an animal against intrusion by others of the same species, and home range as an area used by an individual (or group) but not defended. It seems to me that *Hyla septentrionalis* shows a third sort of spatial orientation, which might be called "home base." The three South American turtles in the room show similar behavior, each usually being found, day after day, in the same place. I presume these turtles, in nature, dig burrows (as does the Florida gopher turtle). Any animal making regular use of a burrow would necessarily show "home base" behavior. The protectively colored forms, like *Phyllomedusa*, do not need to have a regular hiding place.

I suspect that an animal with a home base would also have a home range, since it would need to have a good knowledge of local geography to find its way to the same hiding place each day. The question then becomes, Do animals that show no regular home base, such as the green tree frogs, have a home range to which they restrict their wandering? I don't know, and so far I have been defeated in my attempts to track them.

I bought a dozen small green tree frogs (*Hyla cinerea*) from an animal dealer and released them in the Mango Room. With that number I hoped that I would have both sexes and that they would breed, but I have never found any tadpoles. A herpetological friend told me that they were probably all males, because the usual method of collecting them is by tracking down the calls, which are made only by the males. Certainly they make a tremendous racket in the evening — a visitor once asked if I had geese out there. They are very hard to find, but judging by the continuing noise a number of them must still be there after three years. One took up residence in a small bird house my son made for me and often in the evening could be seen sitting outside on his front porch, looking very cute. That would seem to be a case of home base that lasted for several months.

Anyone who has spent much time in Puerto Rico has heard the coquí (*Eleutherodactylus portorricensis*), a local tree frog that gets its name from its loud, bird-like call, usually of two notes — co-*quí* — the second syllable louder and almost an octave higher. I collected about twenty of them one time in a friend's garden in the outskirts of San Juan and brought them home. They have adapted beautifully to the greenhouse. This species does not have a free tadpole stage — a fully formed tiny frog hatches directly from the egg. I have not found any egg masses in the greenhouse, but I know they are breeding because I have seen the tiny frogs. The coquís often sound off all night long. Visitors are invariably astonished to learn that the call is from a frog, not a bird. I can't identify individual frogs, but I am reasonably sure that they also have home bases, because the calls will come from the same points night after night.

Most of the frogs spend the daytime hiding in bromeliads —plants of the pineapple family which form a characteristic feature of the rain forest everywhere in tropical America.

Since my garden is an "experimental rain forest" I have made a special effort to collect bromeliads — and not just for the benefit of the frogs.

MARSHES IN THE TREETOPS

6

MY INTIMATE ACQUAINTANCE WITH bromeliads started while I was studying the epidemiology (natural history) of jungle yellow fever, which meant that I spent a great deal of time in the jungle — or, as I would prefer to call it, the rain forest. It turned out to be a fascinating place. We tried to keep our eyes on the ball — on yellow fever — but this was hard because of the many distractions.

Among other things, we collected all the different kinds of mosquitoes we could find, whether or not it seemed likely that they were involved in yellow fever: we found nearly 150 species within a radius of about ten miles around the laboratory. There are only 125 species of mosquitoes in all of North America north of the Rio Grande, which makes a nice demonstration of the richness of the tropical fauna. Mosquitoes are apt to be much more numerous in a New Jersey salt marsh or a Michigan bog than in a tropical forest; but in the north the swarms of mosquitoes would all be of one or two species, while in the tropics there would often be many kinds flying — and biting — at the same time and place.

This multiplicity of kinds of mosquitoes reflected a multiplicity of kinds of breeding places. There were, of course, ponds, streams, puddles, swamps — the conventional mosquito habitats. But in the forest there were many other places where water accumulated, and wherever we could find water, we found some species of mosquito breeding. Most of the rot holes in trees held water, as did the bases of palm leaves that had fallen to the ground, or the spathes of palm flowers. There were a number of rather special habitats like the internodes of bamboo where some animal had made a hole permitting water to seep in, and the upright bracts of the flowers of *Heliconia,* a relative of the banana, which held one or two cubic centimeters of water — enough so that each flower was the home of several mosquito larvae. But the most extensive accumulation of water high in the forest canopy was in plants of the pineapple family, the Bromeliaceae.

The bromeliads form a large plant family with almost two thousand species — all American except for one terrestrial species, *Pitcairnia feliciana,* found in 1938 in French Guinea (now the Republic of Guinea). How this lone species made its way into the African forest is anyone's guess; if bromeliads had been in Africa for any length of time, one would think that more than one species would have developed.

Most bromeliads are epiphytic; that is, they grow on the limbs or trunks of trees. They are not parasitic, since they get no sustenance from the host tree; they simply use it as a perch, a place to grow. Some, like the pineapple, are terrestrial, and a few grow on rocks, a habit that the botanists call "saxicolous."

Plants growing as epiphytes have water problems since they cannot reach the soil that provides moisture for terrestrial plants; even in the rain forest rain is intermittent, and there may be periods of many days without showers. As with desert plants, the problem has been solved by various methods of reducing transpiration and of storing water. In the case of bromeliads, a large proportion of the epiphytic species hold water in a "tank" formed by the closely appressed leaf bases: large plants may have five quarts of water or more. Dead leaves and other detritus accumulate in the tanks along with the water, making a rich mixture that is home for a variety of aquatic animals.

The fauna of bromeliads and of other natural water containers has, it seems to me, been unduly neglected. Books on fresh-water biology cover streams, lakes, ponds, marshes and the like, but rarely mention small water accumulations; even rot holes in trees get little attention, although they are common enough in the north and are breeding places for a number of insects, including several species of mosquitoes. The special tropical habitats, like the tanks of bromeliads, are ignored in the books. For me they have the fascination that so often goes with the miniature.

One of the few detailed studies of the inhabitants of

bromeliad tanks was made by Albert M. Laessle on the island of Jamaica (published in the issue of *Ecology* for July 1961). As would be expected, he found numerous protozoa, and was able to identify 15 species with some certainty. Several species of small worms were present, as well as small crustacea. A peculiarity of the Jamaican bromeliad fauna is a special crab, *Metopaulias depressus,* which he found exclusively in these plants and only at elevations above 1,000 feet; he collected as many as 30 specimens from a single large bromeliad. Another species of crab has been reported from bromeliads in Brazil, but in this case the species occupies many other habitats and probably does not breed in the bromeliads.

Insects, understandably, are the most abundant inhabitants of bromeliad tanks. Laessle found a dragon fly and a damsel fly breeding in Jamaican bromeliads; one species of water bug and six of water beetles; and seven species of mosquitoes, as well as eight other kinds of flies. Two species of tree frogs breed in Jamaican bromeliads, and other kinds of tree frogs are often found hiding in the plants, although they do not breed there.

Two tropical American species of *Anopheles* breed in the tanks of bromeliads, and in Trinidad and southern Brazil they have created serious malaria problems in areas where the plants are particularly abundant. Concern about bromeliad malaria has led to some of the most careful ecological and physiological study of the plants. Control has sometimes been attempted by cutting down trees near villages, but the careful use of herbicides is both less drastic and more efficient.

The water and debris of the tanks nourish the bromeliads as well as the animal inhabitants. Special scales on the leaves (called epidermal trichomes) absorb water and nutrients, and the roots of the plants serve only to anchor them to the limbs and trunks of the host trees. In a few species auxiliary roots grow upward into the water and detritus held by the overlapping leaves.

Detritus often accumulates above the water level, and on the outside among the roots. This offers shelter to a considerable variety of non-aquatic animals, so that one can refer to the "terrarium" as well as the "aquarium" aspects of the bromeliad environment. I suspect that those cockroaches that plague our house and furnish food for frogs and lizards in my "experimental rain forest" arrived from Florida nestling in bromeliads. Several species of stinging ants make nests among the roots — a symbiotic or mutual aid relationship, since the plant provides a home for the ants, which in turn protect the plant. Orchids and other epiphytes are also frequently inhabited by ants, making tree-climbing in the tropical forest a hazardous sort of experience.

The pineapple is, of course, the best known of bromeliads. It was widely cultivated by the Indians of the American tropics, where it was encountered by Columbus in 1493 on the island of Guadeloupe. It was spread widely over the world by Spanish and Portuguese colonizers, and it is now grown almost everywhere in the tropics, even on

remote islands of the Pacific. Curiously, the main horticultural varieties were developed early in the last century
by English gardeners growing the plants in glasshouses;
commercial greenhouse cultivation in England disappeared,
however, when it became practical to ship fresh fruit from
places like the Azores.

When I was a boy there were large pineapple plantations
in southern Florida. The industry was ruined, I believe,
by competition from Cuba when the overseas railway was
built to Key West. Now the railway itself is gone, replaced
by a highway; and there is no longer trade between Cuba
and the United States. Our pineapples mostly come from
Hawaii, where they are an important element in the economy; the value of the crop in 1959, according to the *U. S.
Census of Agriculture,* was over thirty-eight million dollars.

Many bromeliads have long been grown as ornamentals
in European greenhouses and conservatories. The flowers
of some are spectacular, and almost all are colorful — mostly
red, pink, lavender or blue, the color being due to prominent bracts rather than to the petals themselves. With some
species, the flowers last for only a few days, but with others
the bracts remain colorful for months. Many species also
have bright berries or variegated foliage.

Bromeliads have become increasingly popular as house
plants in the United States. A Bromeliad Society was
organized in 1950, with headquarters in California. The
society publishes a bimonthly *Bulletin* with articles on
bromeliad culture, on experiences in collecting bromeliads,
on classification, and the like. The cover of each issue has

a color photograph of some interesting member of the family. The *Bulletin* lists nurseries that give special attention to bromeliads. In the issue for April 1969 I find notice of fourteen such nurseries in California, six in Florida and three in Texas. I have brought in all of my plants from Florida nurseries.

Some day bromeliads may be as widely grown as orchids. They seem to me equally interesting and in some respects easier to maintain. Jack Kramer has written a book entitled *Bromeliads: The Colorful House Plants,* based largely on his experience with these plants in his Chicago apartment — showing that it is not necessary to have a greenhouse. Bromeliads have not had nearly as much horticultural attention as have orchids, but a number of hybrids and showy cultivated varieties have been developed. They can be more easily grown from seeds than orchids can — but this is still not a project to be undertaken lightly. Much care and patience is needed, and growth from seed to flower requires several years. Fortunately bromeliads freely produce offshoots or suckers (known as "pups" to bromeliad fanciers), so that vegetative propagation is no problem.

Most people grow even epiphytic bromeliads in pots, using much the same materials and conditions as for epiphytic orchids. It bothers me to see a plant growing in a pot that ought to be growing on the limb of a tree, so I wire my own plants to pieces of branches or of treefern trunks, which I hang from the ceiling of the greenhouse. The plants anchor themselves firmly with their roots in a few months and then present a much more natural appearance.

Sometimes bromeliads go for long periods without flowering, and various methods have been worked out for forcing bloom. Pineapples grown in hothouses in the Azores are forced to bloom at any desired time by keeping the plants in an atmosphere of thick smoke for several days, made by burning straw or other material. This also works for epiphytic bromeliads, but can hardly be recommended for the living room. The gas ethylene also induces blooming, and H. M. Cathey, a horticulturist working in the Beltsville agricultural station in Maryland, has developed a method of forcing flowers by enclosing plants in a plastic bag with slices of apple for four days — the apples give off ethylene. One grower discovered accidentally that the fumes from a pile of manure in his greenhouse caused an unusual number of bromeliads to flower, and several other gases have been found to be effective, including fumes from automobile exhausts.

A number of bromeliads are native to southern Florida, where they are commonly called "air plants." Some of these hold water in which mosquitoes and other insects breed; small frogs and lizards are frequently found hiding in these Florida plants, but none is adapted to breeding there. The well-known Spanish moss of Florida and the Gulf States is a bromeliad, classified by botanists as *Tillandsia usneoides*. The other species of *Tillandsia* have a more orthodox, pineapple-like appearance. The tiny flowers of

Spanish moss, about a quarter of an inch in diameter, are rarely noticed.

Spanish moss grows readily in a greenhouse, producing a nice, tropical effect. I have been unable to get it established in my place, however, because the birds pull it apart to use as nesting material — the only plant damage that I can pin on the birds for a long time. The fiber has been popular as a stuffing for upholstery and mattresses. In the West Indies it is sometimes used as a styptic pad to stop bleeding. Dr. C. W. Mayo of the Mayo Clinic found that it was more absorbent than cotton, taking up "from six to ten times its dry weight in water." It seems, however, never to have found favor with physicians.

I have twenty-two species of bromeliads growing in the greenhouse. I would dearly love to have some of the associated fauna, but I haven't yet figured out how to do it. I don't think the quarantine people would approve of my bringing in tropical mosquitoes, even though there would be no possibility of their surviving in Michigan in the wild — and anyway the birds would probably eat them. Maybe some day I can make a trip to Jamaica and get the special bromeliad crab and frogs — but there is no way of predicting whether they could be established or not. We have encountered all sorts of unexpected difficulties with animals in the garden, and it may be instructive to review some of them.

DEATH IN THE GARDEN

7

WHEN I HAD THE IDEA OF FORMING AN experimental rain forest, I think I had visions of a sample ecosystem with trees and shrubs and all sorts of tropical animals living happily together. Of course I knew that some things were out. One of my favorite animals is the coatimundi — a South American relative of the raccoon — and when I saw one in a pet shop I was very tempted to buy it. But coatis are both inquisitive and bright and stick their long noses into everything; they would tear up plants, kill any small animals and in general reduce the place to shreds. Imagine what a raccoon would do in a greenhouse — and coatis are even more ingenious.

The clever South American capuchin monkeys also turn up frequently in pet shops, but I have resisted any temptation to rescue them. They are the kind of monkey that used to accompany organ-grinders (are organ-grinders totally extinct?), and they are unquestionably the brightest of all monkeys. But there are situations in which intelligence is undesirable. I still vividly remember the scene in the Colombian yellow fever laboratory when a capuchin named Roberta somehow got out to spend the night in the animal-house kitchen. She must have had a splendid time: the walls and even the ceilings were splashed with eggs that had been thrown, vegetables were torn to bits, everything possible was upset and spilled.

People often ask me if I have any snakes. The answer is no. It would be fun to have some of those long, slender, green tropical tree snakes, but all snakes are predators, and I realized that possible predators on small birds, frogs and lizards could not be kept with their prey. But the "garden" turned out to be full of hazards that I had not anticipated. Nancy checks the bird population almost every morning, and we always get worried when it takes a while to locate some individual — and a few of the birds are very good at lurking inconspicuously in the bushes.

One of my first actions was to ask an animal dealer in Colombia to send me a collection of such small lizards and frogs as might be easily available. An amazingly diversified collection of "herps" turned up presently at the airport — they got through customs in record time because the agent had read *The Forest and the Sea* and remembered my name. We took the collection home and started to unpack and distribute the animals.

There were half a dozen horned frogs (*Ceratophrys calcarata*). All frogs are predators, and this is a rather large species; but somehow I couldn't worry about frogs, and

turned them loose. This species, however, has an extraordinarily large mouth — and can be very quick. One of them
almost immediately seized a lizard, the head hanging out
one side of the enormous mouth, the tail out the other.
The lizard was dead by the time I could pry it out. I gave
the frogs to the museum.

There were also a dozen baby caimans in the collection.
This was too many; but I kept four and gave the others
to students. I fixed a shallow pan under a greenhouse
bench, so they could crawl in or out of the water, and fed
them with canned dog food. Things went well for months.
Then one morning I found the mangled corpse of a hummingbird in their pan. The only thing I can figure out
is that the bird had gone down to bathe, and got snapped
up by one of the caimans — they too can be very quick. So
caimans were eliminated from the ecosystem.

Monkeys have also been a problem with the hummingbirds as I reported in Chapter 2. My only primates now
are the marmosets, Dorothy and Margaret. My chief worry
with them concerns Brunhilde. I think she likes to get
into the Monkey Room because fruit flies accumulate there,
waiting to be hunted. She gets through the beaded screen
by hovering an inch or two above a person's head, going
through the parting of the screen with him. She is easy
enough to get back home, though. I chased her back a
couple of times by waving a broom at her. Now all I have
to do is hold back the beaded screen and stick the broom
out; she obediently flies back where she belongs. Who says
birds are dumb? She is very good at dodging the marmo-

sets; but what if she got out there without being noticed and was left for a while?

Hummingbirds can get into all sorts of trouble. One of our saddest memories is Bronzy. Bronzy disappeared one day and we searched all over for him. I finally came across the corpse in the bottom of an open jar among potted plants on a table. He must have got into the jar, perhaps while chasing fruit flies, and then been unable to get out. Since then any empty jar is always left top down: but it took the tragedy of Bronzy to teach us this lesson. We have also learned to keep aquaria and other water containers full to the brim so that any animal that happens to fall in can easily scrabble out. We have never had any trouble with the fish jumping out.

Then there is the problem of mysterious disappearance — which mostly involves animals that can squeeze through crannies or holes. I got a couple of European titmice once: they are alert and unusually clever birds, and I thought it would be interesting to watch their behavior. I put them in the Monkey Room, where they were very adept at escaping the attentions of the marmosets. But after a few months first one disappeared and then the other. I am sure they were not caught by Dorothy or Margaret because there were no tell-tale feathers. My only explanation is that they slipped through slits in the screens that protect the ceiling vents — the slits are necessary for the mechanism that opens the vents in hot weather and they are not as tight as they should be. This is reasonable by way of hindsight, because titmice nest in tree-holes and such places, sometimes with entrances that are very narrow.

The titmice are my only experience with squeezing birds, but I have learned that I cannot keep arboreal lizards in the greenhouse part of the set-up. I once turned loose a number of the Florida anoles ("chameleons") out there, and found that they slipped through the slits in the screens with the greatest of ease. Witness a call from neighbors about strange lizards on their front porch. Lizards are now kept in the Orchid Room — the glassed-in porch from which there is no escape except by squeezing under the door into the Monkey Room. This occasionally happens, to the delight of the marmosets.

I came across a flying squirrel once in a pet shop, found it irresistible, and brought it home. I had visions of establishing a night life in the garden — making it a 24-hour operation, as outside in nature. This was a mistake: the flying squirrel would go tearing around at night, performing all sorts of marvelous acrobatic feats, but also continually disturbing the poor birds who were trying to get their sleep. Fortunately, this didn't last long, because the squirrel presently found his way through one of those slits in the screen to the outside world where he could join his kind in the trees. Night life in the garden now is confined to tree frogs, geckos and cockroaches. The tree frogs sometimes are noisy enough, but mere noise doesn't seem to bother the sleeping birds.

The problem of small mammals for the experimental rain forest has never been solved. Early in the game, I got a couple of pairs of cotton rats (*Sigmodon hispidus*); these range from the southern United States to Argentina, and so would be perfectly appropriate running around on the forest floor. The rats flourished; they dug chambers and tunnels through the sand under the tiles. But they also took to climbing up on the benches and chewing plants and I decided they had to go. When we trapped them, we found that the four had multiplied to eighteen.

We rescued a small chipmunk from a cat and put it in with the marmosets. The chipmunk got along fine until one day he got out into the Mango Room with the birds and tore up a nest the zebra finches had built in a papaya tree, breaking the eggs. So I trapped the chipmunk and released him to the outside world where his destructiveness would be less conspicuous.

We have a history of trouble with zebra finches. They are amusing little birds and ought to be easy to keep. Supposedly they breed readily in captivity, but ours have never made it. They are inveterate nest builders and cause some damage to plants in collecting material, but nothing very serious. Our last male, named Gary because he was so garrulous, managed somehow to hang himself with a strand of Spanish moss.

We had one other loss through hanging: Ethel, a honey-creeper, succeeded in tying one leg to an electric wire with a piece of string. I got her untangled, but she never recovered the use of the leg and finally died about a month after the accident.

The record for the garden is far from being entirely tragic — I am writing here about the failures. My first birds were the Gould's violet-eared hummingbirds, Gamon and Spinach, which I got in March 1965. They are still very much with us, and they still spend a great deal of time quarreling with each other — living together for four years has not resulted in any notable increase in tolerance. The possible longevity of hummingbirds came as a surprise to me: they live their lives at such a fast pace that one would not expect them to be able to continue for long. To be sure, they cannot do without food for any length of time. I remember a shipment of birds from a friend in Los Angeles that had been almost six hours without food by the time I got them home. They were all very faint, unable to fly, but they revived quickly enough when I stuck their bills into tubes of sugar water.

Of course hummingbirds do drop their temperature and go into a sort of torpor at night. Perhaps this daily deep sleep is what keeps them going. At least there are now a number of records of hummingbirds living for eight years or more in captivity. There is no way of knowing the age of hummingbirds captured in the wild, so the captive longevities are minima.

I am often asked if I feel bad about keeping all these animals shut up. The answer is no. I see no signs of cage miseries out in the garden, no attempts at escape beyond incidents I have mentioned here. In most cases when an animal has got in trouble, it seems more from curiosity than from escape behavior. None of the birds pays any attention to the doors — except Brunhilde, and in her case

it seems to be pure wanderlust, or a search for better
fruit-fly hunting.

Zoo directors are often bothered by people who consider that it is morally wrong to keep wild animals in
confinement — in the United States it is illegal to keep
native birds in cages without a special permit. I think this
attitude is based on a sort of anthropomorphism: people
are generally unhappy when shut up in prison, so animals
must be too. It is hard to see the logic of this in modern
zoos; careful studies have been made of the space, diet and
exercise requirements of different species and every effort
is made to meet these. Zoo personnel tend to be as enthu-
siastic animal lovers as could be found and often regard
their charges with great affection — which can hardly be
said of attendants in human prisons.

In the wild much of the time of any animal is spent in
finding food, and in avoiding becoming food for some other
animal. In captivity both of these problems are solved since
food and protection are both provided. The result is a
nice, safe, easy life which seems perfectly satisfactory for
many kinds of animals. I don't like to see birds and mammals in small cages — but I am inconsistent, because I don't
mind seeing fish in a small aquarium. And birds like canaries
seem as well adapted to cage life as guppies are to aquaria.

It is only under the protected conditions of captivity
that animals can reach their maximum life-span, since in
the wild very few animals die of old age. With the accumulation of data from banding, we have information on the
longevity of many birds in nature. Heini Hediger, the

director of the Zurich Zoological Gardens, in his book *Wild Animals in Captivity,* quotes figures for four common British birds. The greatest age for the song thrush in an aviary is 17 years, in the wild 9; for the blackbird the figures are 20 and 10; for the starling, 15 and 9; for the robin, 20 and 11. The average age for all of these birds in the wild is about a year and a half. Thus if length of life is a positive good, captive birds are much better off than wild ones.

CAPTIVES AND CULTIGENS

8

Every once in a while I become enamored of some technical term. "Cultigens" is a good example. I would use it to replace the awkward phrase "cultivated plants and domesticated animals," including any kind of organism maintained by man and genetically modified to fit human needs or whims through the process that Darwin called "artificial selection."

The word was coined by that well-known horticulturist, the late Liberty Hyde Bailey, to cover kinds of cultivated plants for which no wild ancestor was known. Lately, however, a number of anthropologists and geographers have started using the term in a much wider sense, which seems to me useful. I don't see the point in limiting its application to species of unknown ancestry. Often whether or not the ancestry is known is a matter of debate or opinion. Look at the dog, the oldest and one of the best studied of man's cultigens. One can argue that the domestic species is descended from some now-extinct kind of canine, from one of the living wild species, or from a mixture of several types (this last seeming most probable to me).

I like "cultigen" because of the various games that are possible with the word. Species that have become so modified that they can no longer survive without human help can be classed as "obligate cultigens." Maize is one of these; how could it get along without people to husk the ears, remove and sow the seeds? Plants and animals that can escape from human care to run wild would then be "facultative cultigens" — a nicely elegant phrase.

Cultigens by definition are closely associated with man. Before looking at them in more detail it may be useful to consider the other groups of organisms that share this characteristic — the animals, plants and microbes that make up "the human entourage." Cultigens for the most part form an easily distinguished category, but they do at times blur with the organisms that are kept or raised by man, but that have not been genetically modified by this process. Most zoo lions are descended from zoo ancestors, but I would hardly call them cultigens, tame and innocuous as they may be. Then there is the problem of what to call the animals trapped in the wild and sold in our pet shops; or the wildflowers that we often plant in our gardens.

At one time I tried to distinguish the forms that had not been genetically modified through human action as "pets." This system would make kittens "cultigens" and cacti growing in a rock garden "pets." I am ready to give up on that. The meaning of "pet" as an animal kept for pleasure rather than utility is too firmly established and too useful. Dogs, cats, lambs, raccoons, monkeys, parrots — all may be pets. I suppose house plants could also reasonably be included.

What, then, should we call the animals and plants that man keeps purposively, but that he has not modified through breeding? "Captives" is about the best I can do. This term would cover both the animals in zoos and the plants in botanic gardens, as well as the monkeys in New York apartments and the parrots in forest huts. Most of the animals and plants in my "experimental rain forest" are captives rather than cultigens, which is one of the things that have got me interested in the sort of modifications brought about by human manipulation.

Man acquires cultigens and captives on purpose. But there are also many animals that move in on man whether he wants them or not — like the cockroaches in our house. It seems to me that the best word for this group of animals is "inquilines," a word first proposed for the various special insects that make their homes in the nests of ants, bees and termites. Man's inquilines include a variety of insects and sundry kinds of rats and mice.

The inquilines live with man, and indirectly off him as well, feeding on refuse, garbage — and stored food when they can get at it. There are also many organisms that use man himself as food: bedbugs, lice, fleas and a whole catalogue of worms, fungi, protozoa, bacteria and viruses. These are easily labeled "parasites."

Man's entourage also includes a considerable variety of

animals and plants that are only indirectly associated with him — taking advantage of the "open habitat" created by clearing and planting land. Squirrels belong here, as well as various birds with habits like those of the American robin. The plants that we call "weeds" depend on man to clear space for them. Such organisms might be called "opportunists," since they take advantage of the opportunities resulting from human activities.

But I started to write about cultigens before getting off on this more general problem of classification. The origins of our major crop plants and food or draft animals are lost in prehistory, and while a host of experts — archeologists, geneticists, geographers and various kinds of botanists and zoologists — have become concerned with how agriculture may have got started, we shall probably never be sure about the beginnings.

The geographer Carl Sauer, in his book *Agricultural Origins and Dispersals,* has suggested that a settled and secure way of life was necessary for the discovery of cultivation and domestication, noting that people living in the shadow of famine simply do not have time for the sort of experimentation that was necessary. He remarks that "The saying that necessity is the mother of invention largely is not true." He thinks that agriculture was probably first developed by fishing folk living in a mild climate — most likely somewhere in southeast Asia.

The curious thing is that within historic times we have not developed any major new sources of animal or plant food. Did our ancestors discover all of the possibilities?

Or have we lost contact with nature and ceased to explore and experiment, despite our vaunted knowledge and scientific methods? We have, to be sure, made great advances in agricultural productivity in recent years through the application of science and technology — but the improvements have involved traditional crops and animals. A number of people have recently suggested that the meat production of African savannahs would be considerably greater using the diverse native fauna, rather than replacing it with imported cattle as has been the practice. But I know of no large-scale experiments with the breeding and management of such animals.

There are three areas, however, in which we have been acquiring new cultigens in modern times: garden flowers, laboratory animals and tropical fishes. These three groups of organisms are almost completely ignored in the standard books on the origins of cultigens, though I should think studies of them might throw light on the nature of domestication.

I find the neglect of the history of garden flowers particularly puzzling. There is a fine little book by A. W. Anderson, first published in 1951 and currently reprinted by Dover Publications, called *How We Got Our Flowers*, but it deals mostly with modern exploration and with horticultural achievements. What kind of flower gardens did the Greeks and Romans have; or the ancient Chinese and Japanese, since their modern descendants are so much devoted to gardening? What flowers grew in those hanging gardens of Babylon?

Garden books and encyclopedias seem to me to be remarkably negligent of history, except for developments in
modern times, and I have been largely frustrated in my
attempts to find out about ancient gardens. Flowers are, to
be sure, trivial from the point of view of world or local
economy, and it may be for this reason that they are not
often mentioned by writers — flowers are more apt to be
taken for granted than basic foodstuffs.

My concern with the history of flowers may partly come
from experiences in Micronesia and Polynesia. Flowers,
on these Pacific islands, play an important role in the
culture. On the atoll of Ifaluk, where I spent some months,
the women seemed to spend as much time tending flowers
as they did cultivating taro, their basic starch. When they
came in from the gardens, along with the foodstuffs they
would bring baskets of flowers, which were carefully woven
into elaborate garlands. They brought us fresh garlands
to wear every morning. We felt a little foolish about this
at first, but soon became addicted, fixing a mirror on a post
of the chiefs' clubhouse, where we lived, so that we could
be sure our flowers were properly arranged before we
sallied forth for the day. I missed those fresh flowers for
my hair when I came back to the United States; our culture
is unreasonably repressive of male impulses toward orna-
mentation. Maybe the current trend toward gaudy dress
on the part of our young will remedy this.

I remember thinking that if the people of Ifaluk lived
in the United States, they would be ardent members of
the local garden club. Their interest in flowers, however,

was primarily owing to their use in adornment; flowers were like beads or tattooing or pieces of clothing. There seemed to be no interest in growing them as ornamentals around the household areas, no admiration for flowers as a part of the vegetation. This may be a general attitude on the part of "primitive" or "uncivilized" man. Anthropologists tell me that the North American Indians are not known to have cultivated any plants for their flowers; and in general I suspect that feathers and other bright objects are used as ornament more often than flowers, though I have no statistics.

The use of flowers as garlands is not confined to the Pacific, however. Anderson notes that "In Athens Carnations and Violets were the best beloved of all flowers and were worn as garlands at weddings and other ceremonial occasions, and when the main features of the Greek culture were transplanted to Rome these flowers were included." Violets and poppy seeds were also a favorite Roman cure for headaches. This brings up the fact that many of our flowers were first cultivated for their presumed medicinal value. Lilies, for instance, appear in the early herbals because of their value in healing wounds and curing a range of internal disorders — with no mention of their appearance.

It looks to me as though general interest in ornamental gardens in the Western world started with the explorations of the sixteenth century, when travelers began bringing new plants back to Europe from all parts of the world; and that it got a great boost from the interest in nature that developed with the French Enlightenment. Garden history in the Near and Far East, of course, is distinct and different; and many of our flowers were long cultivated there before they were brought to Europe by returning travelers. The tulip craze of the seventeenth century, for instance, was started by the discovery of this flower in a garden near Constantinople by a Viennese, O. G. de Busbecq, in 1554. By 1643, "tulipomania" had reached epidemic proportions in the Netherlands. Anderson quotes an anonymous writer to the effect that "The gaudy Tulip was an object which at one time drove the grave, the prudent and the ambitious Dutchman as wild as ever did the South Sea Bubble the gullible John Bull."

The possibility of growing ornamentals was increased immensely by the perfection of the glasshouse in the nineteenth century. I once calculated that Liberty Hyde Bailey, in his volume *Hortus Second,* published in 1941, which is a list of plants then in cultivation, included 19,600 species. These were perhaps mostly grown in greenhouses in the north, or outdoors in California, Florida and Hawaii, and most of them would be captives rather than cultigens. Horticulturists ransack the world for orchids, bromeliads and other possibly ornamental plants. The hybridization and selection of these tropical plants has become a hobby with many and a considerable business with others. We have not achieved the gambling craze of the Dutch tulip period; but we have a considerable array of special horticultural societies with journals, lectures, garden shows and prizes.

I have learned a lot about plants from trying to grow

things in my greenhouse. I have been particularly impressed by problems with seeds. I had thought that seeds
were something you put in soil and left a while for
germination. But I found that with seeds collected from
various rain-forest plants, germination was both uncertain
and haphazard. While thumbing through the journal
Evolution, I came across an article in the issue for December 1961 by Charles Rick and Robert Bowman, entitled
"Galápagos Tomatoes and Tortoises." The authors had
vainly tried to germinate seeds of a species of wild tomato
from the Galápagos Islands. Finally they fed the tomatoes
to some of the giant tortoises from the islands and collected
the seeds from the feces; after tortoise digestion, they germinated fairly well. The authors then tried a number of
chemical experiments with the seeds; they found that the
seeds would germinate after soaking for half an hour in
50 per cent solution of household Clorox just as well as
after being digested by tortoises.

I immediately tried soaking some of my tropical seeds
in Clorox — in some cases with good results, in others
with continuing failure. There is, I find, a considerable
literature on the chemistry of seed germination, and I intend
presently to go on with experiments with tropical forest
seeds. When you think of it, it is reasonable to find that
seeds of wild plants germinate irregularly; if seeds of a
particular species all germinated in response to a given
stimulus, a climatic catastrophe could wipe out a whole
generation. It is also reasonable to have germination dependent on exposure to digestion by some animal, since

in that way seeds get transport to different environments.

Franz Schwanitz, in a book on *The Origin of Cultivated Plants,* notes "the loss of delayed germination" as one of the characteristics of plant cultigens. Other characteristics are: giantism, reduction or loss of natural means of dissemination, loss of bitter and toxic substances, loss of mechanical means of protection (thorns, for instance, and prickly fruits), simultaneous ripening of fruits and the like. The expectation that seeds will germinate promptly and uniformly is, then, a consequence of dealing with cultigens. Seeds of our common northern wildflowers may take as long as two years to germinate, or may require special treatment such as freezing.

These cultigens, captives, inquilines, parasites and opportunists that make up the human entourage form one aspect of our environment. But the whole complex set of relationships between man and other organisms and between man and the physical world is best looked at as forming the "human ecosystem."

THE HUMAN ECOSYSTEM

9

ONE GETS THE IMPRESSION, THESE DAYS, that everyone has become aware of the environment. The President makes speeches about the quality of the environment; the Mayor of New York has discovered air (Los Angeles discovered it long ago); the Department of Health, Education and Welfare has started work on a gigantic center located in North Carolina for the study of environmental health. There have been endless committees, commissions, conferences and symposia, all producing reports. I have a large pile of the reports here in my study, with titles like "The Dynamic Spectrum: Man, Health and Environment"; "Environmental Quality in a Growing Economy"; "Air Pollution"; "Waste Management and Control"; "An Ecological Approach to Environmental Stress." There are dozens more, but that should give the idea.

Of course the environment is not new, nor is awareness of man's effect as an agent of environmental deterioration.

The classic book on the subject, *Man and Nature; or Physical Geography as Modified by Human Action,* by George Perkins Marsh, was published in 1864. It was reissued in 1965 by Harvard University Press, with a historical and biographical introduction by David Lowenthal. Marsh's book was widely read in the latter part of the nineteenth century, and it had considerable influence on the thinking of many people. Among other things, it led directly to the establishment of our forest reserves. Former Secretary of the Interior Udall has well said that it marked "the beginning of land wisdom in this country." The book still reads easily, with an up-to-date feeling except for occasional anachronisms like remarks about malaria being caused by bad air.

Yet our wisdom about the environment, about the land we inhabit, sometimes seems not to have shown much growth in the hundred years since Marsh published his book. In fact, the current outpouring of reports, studies, plans and laws is an indication that environmental deterioration is reaching crisis proportions. We seem to require a crisis before starting to take effective action — which makes one wonder about all this talk of man as a "rational animal."

Environment — I can remember when I thought it was a rather simple idea. It meant the setting, the surroundings, of an individual, a population, or a biological community. But the more I have thought about it, the more confused I have become, which is a not unusual consequence of concentrating on some particular idea. One difficulty is that organisms and their environments form interacting systems, modifying each other in varied ways. The type of forest, for instance, that grows in a particular region depends in part on the regional climate and soil; but the type of soil is also a consequence of the kind of forest (coniferous, hardwood, or what) and the presence of the forest results in modification of the climate. These sorts of relations have led ecologists increasingly to try to think in terms of *ecosystems:* of living organisms and physical factors in the environment forming parts of interrelated wholes.

When we turn to man, then, we would do well to think not so much about the human environment as about the human ecosystem. An increasingly large proportion of the earth's surface is being altered by human actions — and this in turn is coming to govern what men do or can do. Ecologists, who tend to be fond of big words, sometimes call this man-dominated region of the globe the "anthroposere"; or, following a Russian named Vernadsky, the "noösphere," the world of the mind which is coming to replace the "biosphere," the world of life. I dislike both of these words, and prefer to think about "the man-altered landscape," though I do wish I had a better phrase.

The human ecosystem involves a particularly puzzling and complex set of interrelations among its organic and inorganic components. I first became fully aware of this when I was asked, a few years ago, to talk about "the environment" with one of the national committees that had been formed to consider our resource problems. I made a fairly conventional sort of analysis in terms, particularly, of the perceptual environment (the aspects of the world about us that we are able to intercept and interpret with our sense organs) and the operational environment (things that affect us physically even though we cannot directly perceive them; viruses and some kinds of radiation, for instance). When I had finished, an anthropologist who was present, Peter Murdock, asked, "What do you do about the supernatural environment?"

This gave me pause. I had recently spent some time on an atoll in Micronesia where spirits were very common. They were as "real" to the people as, say, the sharks in the lagoon—and far more important because they could, if not properly propitiated, do a great deal more damage, by calling up a typhoon or causing an epidemic. We, with our background of Western science, knew that the spirits were not really there; they were creations of the minds of the people. But their influence on human behavior, as a part of the atoll environment, was undeniable.

Discussion of Murdock's idea rapidly became general. We did not believe that there were any spirits lurking in the Board Room of the National Academy of Sciences, where we were meeting. But we soon realized that the place teemed with various ideas and attitudes that the individuals present had acquired from their cultural backgrounds — we were really in no position to feel superior to the Micronesians. I think it was the botanist Ray Fosberg who suggested that we should talk, not about the "supernatural environment," but about the "conceptual environment": the world of ideas that surrounds every man and that so greatly influences his beliefs and behavior.

This brings us back to the ecosystem, to a special case

of the interaction of organism and environment. Our culture — which I presume is the conventional term for our conceptual environment — is developed by people, perhaps in part by individuals, but more by the accumulated traditions of groups. We made it; but it in turn molds our actions, our way of life.

Sometimes I visualize this most easily in terms of clothing and housing. What we wear is determined by our ideas of what we ought to wear: only in such cases as space suits and arctic garments has practicality won over appearance. Many studies have shown that from the point of view of comfort and physiology, the ideal clothing for the wet tropics is no clothing. But even when we move into this environment we cling to our ideas of propriety, and find it easier to change the climate with air conditioning than to take off our clothes. This is a particularly sore point with me because I hate the tight feeling of a necktie: yet on the lecture platform or at a committee meeting, there I am, following the laws of convention. At least it enables me to make the point sometimes about the compelling influence of the conceptual environment on human behavior and physical comfort.

Lynn White, Jr., professor of history at the University of California, Los Angeles, has published a most thought-provoking article in the issue of *Science* for March 10, 1967, entitled "The Historical Roots of Our Ecologic Crisis." He sketches developments in the history of the Judeo-Christian tradition that have led to our present worship of science and technology — and to the present crisis in our relations with the rest of nature. White feels that today's patching and mending is, in the long run, futile without some large change in our attitude — in our religion.

"There are many calls to action," he writes, "but specific proposals, however worthy as individual items, seem too partial, palliative, negative: ban the bomb, tear down the billboards, give the Hindus contraceptives and tell them to eat their sacred cows . . . What shall we do? No one yet knows. Unless we think about fundamentals, our specific measures may produce new backlashes more serious than those they are designed to remedy." We need, in terms of my phraseology, to modify our conceptual environment.

In the meanwhile we are living — and in the course of our summer vacations we will be traveling — in a man-altered landscape that is the consequence of our ideas. The supremacy of the automobile, the pattern of highways and towns and cities, the forests that are gone and those that are left as parks or reserves, the animals that are protected and those that are persecuted — our whole ecosystem has been shaped by the concepts of our culture.

This ecosystem is curiously neglected as a subject of scientific study. Ecology and economics have the same Greek root (from *oikos*, the household). Yet when one looks at the textbooks and college courses, there is almost nothing in common. When I wrote *The Forest and the Sea* back in 1960, I made the quip that ecologists like to play the game of pretending that man doesn't exist, while economists, correspondingly, like to pretend that nature doesn't exist. There is an increasing amount of communication between the two groups — though we still have a long way to go before we achieve any real understanding of the problems of man and nature.

The ecologists are beginning to discover the man-altered landscape, and I have attended a number of meetings on the subject — always getting new ideas, and sometimes new words. I am especially fond of some of the words. There is, for instance, the "suburban forest" that stretches along the eastern seaboard from somewhere north of Boston to the suburbs of Washington. The forest tends to be continuous, surrounding the cemented islands of the cities themselves, and a whole series of animals (opportunists) have adapted nicely to life in this habitat: a variety of birds and such mammals as squirrels, opossums, raccoons and even skunks. I have thought that many of these animals should be grateful to people — squirrels in particular, since they are so much more abundant and well fed there than in other types of forest.

And then I remember at a conference in Connecticut someone using the phrase "derelict woodland" for the growth on abandoned farms and for the forests along the rivers badly cut over in the last century for firewood for the river boats. In the case of Connecticut, one third of the area is now under cultivation or taken over by cities or suburbs; one third has been cleared but is now abandoned, and the other third has been cut over but never completely cleared. What to do about this "derelict woodland" that covers two thirds of Connecticut is somewhat of a puzzlement — should it be managed or left alone?

I picked up a new phrase the other day from an official of one of our western states who did not think much of the primeval forest. "Decadent forest," he called it: littered with unused and rotting logs: quiet, dark, with its animal life unapparent, at least to the casual visitor. Man, he felt, could do a great deal to improve this sort of situation by cleaning the place out.

We are concerned with a question of values: some people like the man-made environment of cities as a permanent way of life, others like to escape when they can, and still others are perfectly happy without ever going near a city. We need more study of the psychological factors involved, as well as of the physical effects of pollution of air, water and soil. But we need to know more about all aspects of the man-altered landscape, because this, after all, is the world in which most of us are forced to spend our lives.

Lynn White, in the article I quoted earlier, suggested that Saint Francis of Assisi should be the patron saint of ecologists. "The key to an understanding of Francis," White writes, "is his belief in the virtue of humility — not merely for the individual but for man as a species. Francis tried to depose man from his monarchy over creation and set up a democracy of all God's creatures." Unfortunately Saint Francis failed. "Both our present science and our present technology are so tinctured with orthodox Christian arrogance toward nature that no solution for our ecologic crisis can be expected from them alone."

But the answer, immensely difficult though it is, seems simple. Our troubles stem from our conceptual environment. We made it. All we have to do is to change it!

Visitors to the experimental rain forest are likely to be
greeted by Brunhilde, one of several hummingbirds.

Photo by Ralph Fertig.

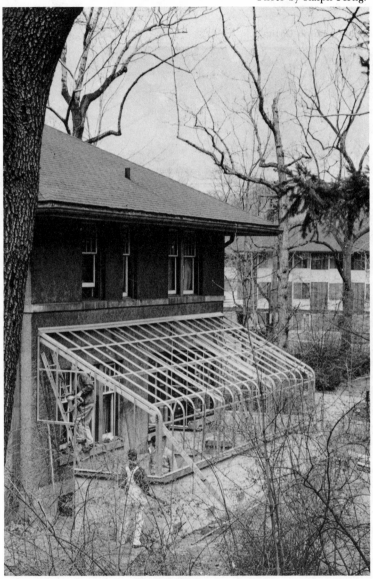

Building the greenhouse: the left-hand end will be
the Mango Room; to the right the Monkey Room.
Inside the house, to the right, is the Orchid Room.

A view of the Mango Room.

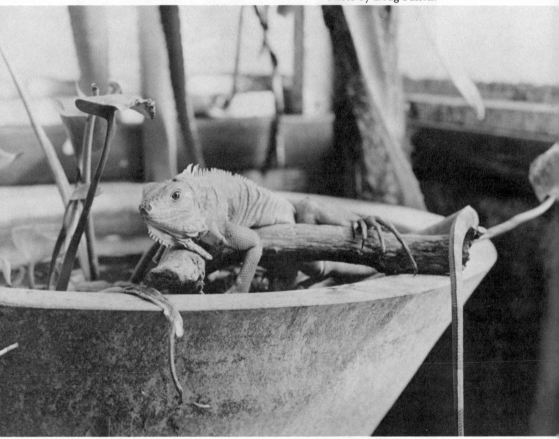

Héloïse. Iguanas spend a great deal of time doing nothing at all.

Scrounge, the blue-backed manakin.

Jan, a golden-eared tanager.

Bronzy, a hummingbird from Ecuador.

Two Ecuadorean tanagers at the feeding station.

Dorothy, a marmoset, and a bromeliad in bloom.

Home base for one of the frogs.

EATING AND BEING EATEN

10

SOMETIMES I HAVE THOUGHT THAT I missed my profession — that I should have been a filing clerk. At least I love to make catalogues and work out systems of classification. On the other hand, maybe it is just as well that I don't have professional status, since my systems never seem to work very well — which, of course, doesn't keep me from trying. For years now I have been attempting, off and on, to find ways of analyzing the human ecosystem. There is the problem of trying to classify the different habitats, from cemented cities to maintained nature reserves. And then there is the different problem of working out a scheme of categories for the different kinds of relationships that have come to exist between the human animal and other organisms. There are many complications; but one category is fairly clear — food. Eating and being eaten.

Our pre-human ancestors, the protohominids, must have

been integral parts of the biological communities in which they lived. The structure of the biological community depends on who eats whom — the transference of energy from the producing green plants, through the "key industry animals" that live directly off the plants and the various predators and parasites that eat these, and so to the decomposers who return the materials of the corpses again to dust. There are many lines of evidence to indicate that the protohominids were social carnivores, living in hunting packs able to cope with ever larger and more diverse kinds of game as they acquired tools and skills.

The role of the protohominids in the community would thus be comparable with that of wolf packs, differing considerably from that of the living primates that we know, who are mostly vegetarian or insectivorous, or general scroungers of whatever they can collect and digest. I suspect the protohominids were scroungers too, supplementing their meat diet with nuts, berries, tubers, grubs, eggs and the like. They probably also did not scorn jackal-like scavenging: the aversion to "spoiled" meat is a cultural trait not shared, for instance, by the British upper classes, who like their game "high."

Man, or pre-man, was thus probably more miscellaneous in his food habits than most predators; but his primary impact on fellow animals was surely as a carnivore. I like the statistics collected by Raymond Dart (published in *Adventures with the Missing Link*) on his study of 7,159 animal fragments found associated with australopithecine fossils in a cave at Makapansgat in South Africa. He determined that these represented the remains of at least 39 large bucks of kudu and roan antelope size; 126 medium-sized wildebeeste-type antelopes; 100 small gazelle-like animals; and 28 specimens of a tiny, duiker-like species. In addition, there were remains of 4 horses of extinct species; 6 chalicotheres (an extinct type of tree-browsing creature); 6 giraffes, also of extinct species; 5 rhinos; 1 hippopotamus; 20 wart hogs; and 45 baboons. Bones of porcupines, hares and water turtles were found along with this larger game. Fragments of eggshells show that the australopithecines were addicted to robbing bird nests; and crab shells show that they did not mind eating invertebrates.

So much for the food of the protohominids. How about their being eaten? It is difficult to get an idea of the food habits of early man; but it is far more difficult to estimate his role as food for other animals. Hermann Dembeck, in a fascinating book, *Animals and Men,* cites the opinion of both L. S. B. Leakey and Herodotus to the effect that man was probably not an attractive prey for the big cats — whether living or extinct species. "Perhaps the reason the race of man survived," Dembeck says, "is due to his repulsive smell and the bad taste of his flesh."

That is not a very flattering thought. Maybe the occasional lions and leopards that take to man-eating are simply lacking in discrimination. Some species of crocodiles, at least, take to people whenever they get the chance. While on this subject, it has been suggested that the rarity of attacks on man by the big South American anacondas, perfectly capable of swallowing a calf, may be due to his upright stance, which makes him seem to the snake too big to be managed.

I have always heard that cannibals consider fellow men to be a particularly tasty kind of meat. Cannibalism is also generally presumed to be an ancient human habit, in part because the long bones of the fossils of Pekin Man were split open — and splitting could only be carried out by a fellow man with a tool; other animals would gnaw the bones. Yet Lewis Mumford, in his thought-provoking book *The Myth of the Machine*, uses this as an example of the scholarly habit of jumping to conclusions. He points out that "We have no evidence to indicate whether these creatures were killed or died a natural death. If we suppose they were killed, we do not know if homicide was the custom of the country, or whether this was a particular case. . . . Nor yet do we know if they were killed by their own kind, by another group, or by some more gigantic predatory hominid of a vanished race whose huge teeth were also found in China."

But whatever its history, there is no question that cannibalism has occurred within widely different cultures in historic times: though tribes have probably often enough been accused of cannibalism on the simple theory that "cannibal" and "savage" were roughly equivalent terms. Anthropologists have had a fine time here with classification: there are exocannibals, who eat only enemies; endocannibals, who eat only friends; various sorts of ritual cannibalism, and the like. But this is just another aspect of the fact that man has been his own chief enemy for quite a while.

Man may not, then, have been a common source of food for any predator except possibly fellow man. But he has long provided food for many other kinds of creatures, the organisms we call parasites. He supports a special kind of flea and three species of lice, and contributes to the food supply of a variety of ticks, mosquitoes and other biting insects, as well as maintaining a considerable fauna and flora of worms, protozoa, bacteria, viruses and fungi. The parasitic way of life, in the textbooks, is often described as "degenerate." This has always puzzled me. I suppose, as predators ourselves, we admire other animals of this ilk, and make the lion "king of beasts." But personally I would much rather be bitten by a mosquito than by a lion.

I have been writing about man's food relations — about eating and being eaten — from the biological point of view. I have been writing, in other words, as though culture, ideas, attitudes, tradition did not exist. But the behavior of *Homo sapiens* is always modified by his conceptual environment, and this must go way back in time, perhaps even to those australopithecines studied by Raymond Dart and L. S. B. Leakey. Ideas, however, leave few fossils, and we can only guess at their influence on the food habits of early man. With living peoples the influence is obvious and pervasive. I think one could say that no known culture uses the food materials present in the environment in terms of availability and nutritional value. No culture is entirely "rational" about food.

I remember once in the llanos of eastern Colombia sitting around a fire eating toasted ants — the sexual forms that happened to be swarming in great numbers at that time. They had a pleasant, nutty flavor — and in season were sold at the local movie theater, serving the same function (and having the same effect) as popcorn with us. I happened to remark to my ant-eating friends that in my country people ate the legs of frogs — an idea that they greeted with horror. It was as though I had spoken of some repulsive sexual activity. This may have been the beginning of my interest in the curious parallels between the cultural controls over food and sex — finally resulting in the book entitled *Gluttons and Libertines*.

There is no evidence, as far as I know, that any of the food taboos are based on factual observation of ill effects (I am not classing the avoidance of poisons as "taboos"). It is sometimes said that the Jewish and Moslem taboo on pork has a basis in the danger of infection by trichina. But this looks like reasoning after the fact. It is more likely that the taboo started as a reaction against a heathen pig-cult that was once widespread in the Mediterranean region — only the worshippers of false gods ate pigs. Sometimes it is argued that the avoidance of pork has a basis in the filthy, scavenging habits of pigs; but chickens have equally filthy habits (from our point of view) and are eaten by people who reject pork.

Frederick Simoons has written a book on meat taboos in the Old World with the title *Eat Not This Flesh*. He points out that chickens and eggs are about as widely tabooed as pork, though by peoples who have been less well publicized than the pork-avoiders. This taboo is particularly strong among many African tribes. Chickens most commonly are prohibited for women, but in some tribes they may be prohibited for everyone, or for certain ages and social classes. They are frequently thought to be a cause for sterility, but a variety of other reasons may be given for the avoidance. Chickens and eggs often have religious significance, and chickens may first have been domesticated for purposes of divination rather than for eating. Most commonly prophecy depends on the angle at which bamboo splinters, inserted into the perforations of the thighbone, project. Cockfighting may also have sacred aspects, though cockfighting appears to be a trait of civilizations rather than of primitive tribes.

We are apt to feel superior to people who refuse to eat good food like chicken on superstitious grounds. But we have plenty of food taboos ourselves. One of the strongest of these is the taboo on eating dogs, though in many parts of the world dogs are raised for food, and in classical antiquity roasted puppies were considered a great delicacy.

To show the strength of our present dog taboo, Frederick Simoons cites the case of Lieutenant Andrew O'Meara, who, "to demonstrate means of military survival," killed, skinned and cooked a stray dog on a spit in Peoria, Illinois. He was prosecuted under an Illinois statute against cruelty to animals and given the maximum sentence — even though he killed the dog with a sudden blow. Our colonial ancestors were not so fussy. The Indians ate dogs, and they must frequently have sustained trappers and explorers. Dogs formed the chief meat for members of the famous Lewis and Clark expedition to the Pacific after the party had passed beyond the bison range in the Great Plains, and Clark noted in his journal that the men preferred dogflesh to any of the local game. They bought all the dogs they could from the local Indians, and Paul Russell Cutright in his book *Lewis and Clark: Pioneering Naturalists* remarks that they must have "reduced the dog population of the Columbia River valley appreciably."

CONCERNING CRUD

11

Every ANIMAL MUST EAT — AND EVERY ANImal also produces waste products. Usually the waste of one organism is the food of some other organism in the course of the endless cycling of materials through the biosphere. Man has unusual food habits — cooking, for instance — but his food habits are not nearly so peculiar as his waste habits. And as he becomes more "civilized" (and more numerous), he produces an ever greater variety and volume of wastes, to the point where now he is in imminent danger of irreversibly wrecking the ecological balance of the biosphere and of being suffocated in the accumulation of his own garbage.

"When some future historian shall sit down to summarize what the present generation of Americans has accomplished, his climactic sentence could read, 'Of the waters, they made a cesspool; of the air, a depository for poisons;

and of the good earth itself, a dump where rats nuzzled in piles of refuse.' "

With these words George Stewart starts his book *Not So Rich as You Think*. He goes on to speculate about the need for some one word for all of the miscellaneous effluents of our affluent society. "There does not exist in English — and perhaps not in any other language — any single traditional term covering the whole conception. Instead we all know a host of more or less specific terms — *sewage, garbage, junk, litter, smog, refuse, waste, offal, slops, pollutants, rubbish, trash. . . .* Perhaps the nearest to universality is *crud*, that coinage of the G.I.'s of World War II. But that term is now old-fashioned slang, and in many people's minds approaches being an obscenity."

It is crud, all right, and why not call it that? As for obscenity, the *Oxford English Dictionary* notes that that word probably comes from the Latin *obscenus,* meaning "repulsive, filthy, disgusting." What could be more appropriate?

Stewart's book (aptly illustrated with drawings by Robert Osborn) forms an excellent survey of contemporary American crud production. There is also a fine companion volume, *The Frail Ocean* by Wesley Marx, which takes up the problems of the crud that is accumulating in the seas — which we blissfully regard as the perfect dumping ground because the stuff is at least hidden from our sight under the waves.

Stewart suggests that human messiness comes in part at least from our simian ancestry ("Monkeys cannot be house-broken"). Birds and arboreal mammals can quite simply drop things with the assurance that they are thus removed from the environment. Birds keep their nests clean, but our nest-building ape cousins don't even bother with that. George Schaller, in his well-known study *The Mountain Gorilla*, reports on the examination of 2,451 gorilla nests (they are built anew each night). He found dung in 99 per cent of the nests, and in 73 per cent of the cases there was evidence that the animal had lain on the feces. If this is our background, it is no wonder that we are careless.

We do usually manage to housebreak our children — though some psychologists seem to think we may damage personalities in the process — but the history of human crud disposal is not reassuring. I wonder about those australopithecine cave inhabitants of South Africa. They had come down out of the trees, but it doesn't look as though they had acquired tidy habits. The human fossils are found together with thousands of animal bone fragments — apparently leftovers from food, though Raymond Dart thinks that many bones were used for tools. But what about the australopithecines themselves? Were corpses allowed to rot where they fell? The caves must have been pretty foul-smelling places. When we do find evidence of burial, as with the Neanderthal men, it seems to have been for religious rather than sanitary reasons.

Then came the development of agriculture and the possibility of settled village life — the period known to anthropologists as the Neolithic. "Neolithic man," Stewart observes, "having invented living in permanent villages and keeping cows and sheep, immediately faced a disposal problem. This was one price of his advance toward civilization. Apparently he solved this problem by generally ignoring it." This, of course, was a help to future archeologists, because they could learn much about ways of life from the study of kitchen-middens — the polite term for ancient garbage dumps. Peasant peoples today often live with their animals in a welter of manure and refuse: I remember thinking, when living in Egypt, that the accumulated debris made the average village look as though it had recently suffered a bombing raid.

New disposal problems arose with the concentration of people in cities. Some cities, like those of the Indus Valley, Mesopotamia and Crete, had marvelously constructed sewers and drains; but others must have been extraordinarily filthy. The seven cities at the site of Troy are a case in point — each city built on the debris of its predecessor. The people seemingly never bothered to clear anything away. And so the history continues through the notorious slops and filth of medieval cities.

It seems, then, that man has long lived with his own crud. There are, of course, many shining exceptions. I remember vividly the neatness and cleanliness of the un-Westernized Micronesians on Ifaluk, where I spent part of 1953. But they had the lagoons easily available for bathing and for dumping; and their dumping was too limited to cause any pollution problem. There were no tin cans, no bottles, no paper; and the feces were eaten by fish and thus recycled in the ecosystem.

If most men have been living in their own fouled nests for so long, what is all the fuss about now? There is, in the first place, a matter of sheer quantity. The exploding human numbers result in a corresponding explosion of human waste products. Furthermore, in the United States at least, there is a clear tendency toward increase in the amount of crud per person. In *Man on Earth,* S P R Charter notes that "In 1940 the people of the United States accumulated an average of two pounds of garbage per person per day for a national total of some 50 million tons a year. Twenty years later, in 1960, the garbage averaged a little more than 3.5 lbs. per person per day, for a national total of some 115 million tons a year." I don't know where Charter got his figures, but they sound reasonable.

Stewart lists three other basic causes of the present crisis: the growth of cities, the development of the "affluent society" and the invention of synthetic technology. Seven out of ten Americans now live in metropolitan areas, whereas in the not distant past most were rural, living on farms. On the old-fashioned farm, waste disposal could safely be left to the individual or the family: garbage buried, manure used to fertilize the fields. The city-dweller has no way of disposing of his own waste; there must be some public means of collection and disposal, which means taxes unwillingly paid and generally inadequate.

One characteristic of our affluence, of course, is that things are often thrown away to be replaced by new, instead of being repaired — in our economy replacing is often cheaper than repairing, at least in the short run. And no one seems to worry about the long-term costs. We also rarely recycle materials; they are used and then dispersed. The junk-man has come to represent a rare and not highly respected profession, though in a thrifty economy he would be very important. As Stewart remarks, "Don't shoot the secondary materials man."

We are all aware of the industrial wastes that pollute water and air — though there is little agreement about what to do about them. The synthetic technology, in addition to wastes, turns out a variety of products that are difficult to get rid of. Plastics, for instance: they don't rot or rust, and burn only with a very hot flame. Like glass, the plastics will stay with us to help future archeologists investigating our culture; the plastics don't even break so that they can be converted into pretty pebbles by the pounding surf, as is the case with glass. And then there is the problem of the highly dangerous crud produced by nuclear reactors.

Stewart sometimes sounds as though our crud problems would be solved if we could get the stuff to the ocean; but Wesley Marx points out the dangers there. We tend still to think in terms of Lord Byron's well-known lines:

> Roll on, thou deep and dark blue ocean — roll!
> Ten thousand fleets sweep over thee in vain;
> Man marks the earth with ruin — his control
> Stops with the shore.

But this is no longer true. Even the oceans falter with the load of man's accumulating crud. "Fish stocks can be depleted. The nurseries of marine life can be buried.

Beaches can erode away. Seawater, the most common substance on this earth and the most life nourishing — at once
liquid soil and liquid atmosphere — can be hideously cor-
rupted. It can host substances that in the stomachs of
oysters or clams are refined into poisons that paralyze por-
poise and man alike."

The stories told by Stewart and Marx are dismal indeed.
Even more dismal is the fact that in general we know
what we are doing, and in many cases have the knowledge
and ability to correct our actions, but we are unwilling to
spend the money and the effort until events reach crisis
proportions, when it may be too late. We are running up
a tremendous bill that must be paid by our descendants —
"we are not so rich as you think." Solutions, also, often
require governmental or regional planning and action:
the "government interference" that is viewed so dimly in
the American tradition. In the case of the sea, international
planning is urgently needed, and the control of marine
resources might quite logically be a function of the United
Nations.

It is difficult to be cheerful about the human animal
when we look at his resource management or his methods
of disposing of things. The quip of John Pairman Brown,
in a little book entitled *The Displaced Person's Almanac,*
is all too applicable: "We've converted our rivers into
sewers and our forests into funnybooks; this is our boon
from the Gods, everything we touch turns into garbage."
Maybe he should have said crud.

CROWDED ANIMALS

12

MAN IS UNQUESTIONABLY AN ANIMAL, however peculiar he may be in many of his behavioral characteristics. He has the same kind of innards as other mammals; he needs oxygen, water and food; and however much he may deplore the fact and try to hide it, he produces urine and feces. Reproduction is sexual, though the periodicity that characterizes sex in most animals has been lost.

With this clear animal background in anatomy and physiology, isn't it likely that there is also an animal background to human behavior? The trouble is, of course, that learning is of such overwhelming importance in determining the nature of human actions that any innate background is hard to uncover. And learning, I am sure, can completely reverse possible inherent tendencies. For instance, I like Stewart's idea that a monkey-like inclination to scatter things persists in man: but he certainly can learn to be very neat, orderly and clean. Therein lies the only hope for the solution of the crud problems of our civilization.

There has been a great deal of discussion lately of the possible biological basis of human aggression, which I want to consider in a later chapter. But important as pollution and aggression are in shaping the human ecosystem, they are subordinate to the problem of dizzily multiplying human numbers. It is interesting, in this connection, to look at the biological effects of crowding on animals — and people.

Biologists have been concerned with the study of animal populations ever since the time when Thomas Robert Malthus first enunciated his "dismal theorem." As stated in the 1803 edition of his *Essay on Population,* the Malthusian propositions are, first, that "population is necessarily limited by the means of subsistence," and second, that "population invariably increases where the means of subsistence increase unless prevented by some very powerful and obvious checks." In the case of man, Malthus considered that the checks were all resolvable into "moral restraint, vice and misery."

Malthus was concerned with the human problem; and human populations certainly often behave in accord with the Malthusian propositions. If one used "moral restraint" to cover contraception, abortion, infanticide and continence, one could well argue that they always apply. And if Paul Ehrlich is right in his book *The Population Bomb,* we are all in for a great deal of misery presently because of man's continuing multiplication — and I am afraid that he is right.

But what about other animals? Undeniably the means of subsistence is the ultimate limit on any population; but in natural communities animals rarely live up to this limit. There usually seems to be plenty of food for all, and death through starvation is probably rare. As a graduate student I specialized in the study of our native fruit flies (Trypetidae), and I became impressed with the quantity of wild fruits I had to examine to find a few larvae. Most of this perfectly good fruit-fly food was going to waste! Now I look out the window at the trees, shrubs and grass and think about all the caterpillar fodder that is not being used — even in a situation where no insecticides have been applied.

Where a population does live up to the limit of the means of subsistence, catastrophe is likely to result. The incredible hordes of migratory locusts that at times strip the countryside of every green thing in various parts of the world are a case in point. Locust plagues have been recorded in Egypt and Assyria since the beginning of written history. Disastrous insect outbreaks are often the consequence of man's interference with the ordinary balance of natural communities, but this can hardly be the case with locusts. There is even what might be called a "fossil" locust swarm which became embedded in the ice of the glacier on Mount Cook in Montana in pre-Columbian times. Because of the damage they cause, these insects have received a great deal of attention from entomologists, but there was no explanation of the swarming migratory flights until 1921, when B. P. Uvarov first announced his phase theory.

The migratory locust of the Near East had been classified as a species (*Locusta migratoria*) distinct from a similar solitary grasshopper (*Locusta danica*). The two differed in measurements of head length and width, leg length, and color (*migratoria* being dark and *danica* green), as well as in behavior. Uvarov found that if hoppers were raised under crowded conditions, the adults turned into the migratory form; if they were raised in isolation, the adults were of the solitary form. The two "species" were different phases of the same animal.

Uvarov's theory has been amply confirmed by subsequent work — it has the status of a fact rather than a theory. All of the seven grasshopper species in different parts of the world that sometimes form dangerous locust plagues have been found to show this phenomenon. The solitary forms live dispersed in grasslands, slowly building up abundance until, at some stage in crowding, the restless, gregarious migratory form appears and the great hordes of insects, darkening the sky, take off to devastate any vegetation in their paths. The swarms may fly out to sea; and they almost always end in some environment where the species cannot survive. New swarms are then built up from individuals that stayed behind in the homeland.

The mass suicide clearly serves as a final limit to population growth. But what adaptive value does this behavior have that could lead to the evolution of the two different phases? The most widely held theory is that the migrations are a form of "environment-hopping." The grasshopper species that occasionally form migratory swarms live in arid or semi-arid regions where the environment is never stable for long. The phase change provides a way in which the species can occasionally burst out from one kind of habitat into others. It gives the species two ways of life instead of leaving it chained to one. Most swarms die out, but sometimes populations may become established in new areas, thus promoting the survival and dispersal of the species.

It has recently been found that a number of other kinds of insects show phase changes when raised under crowded conditions. At first it seemed that this might be the explanation of other insect migrations — and the phenomenon does hold true in many cases. Unfortunately some non-migratory species, such as the European emperor moth (*Saturnia pavonia*), which does not even have functional mouth parts as an adult, also show dark phase changes when raised under crowded conditions. There is no one-to-one relation between phase change and gregarious migration in all insects.

A number of species of Lepidoptera, especially in the tropics, show mass gregarious movements that seem to be suicidal. I have stood on the Caribbean coast of Honduras and watched millions of butterflies, several species flying together, streaming out to sea and certain death. Little is known about the background of these mass swarms: the species are of no economic importance, and the population build-ups occur in remote parts of the tropics where there are no entomologists to study them.

The mass suicide of these insects brings to mind the famous case of the Norwegian lemmings. Lemmings are small, mouse-like rodents that inhabit the subarctic regions of both hemispheres. Most species show rather regular cycles of abundance with peaks at intervals of three or four years. This has been the subject of a great deal of study — Charles Elton wrote a book about it, with the title *Mice, Voles and Lemmings* — but we still can hardly be said to understand the cyclic regularity. The Norwegian lemmings have attracted particular attention because in years of abundance they pour down from the mountains toward the sea through farms, villages and towns — indifferent to obstacles and to people.

G. C. Clough has written a first-hand account of a lemming outbreak in Norway, entitled "Lemmings and Population Problems," in the issue of *The American Scientist* for June 1965. "The peak population, which I watched all through the summer," he writes, "began to move downward from the alpine shrub and lichen zones rather suddenly in mid-July. During the short night and early morning hours, I could see individual animals proceeding at a steady pace down along a hiking trail. While I sat at a convenient observation point where a road crossed a small river, as many as forty lemmings per hour passed by. These animals were not heading toward a good wintering ground. In fact, by September and October, when the first snows came, many of them had settled in the large, low-lying marsh and in a hayfield devoid of green grass. None of them survived the winter here. Other wandering lemmings began to appear at the nearest town and surrounding pine forests twelve miles away down the valley."

The migrating lemmings were completely antisocial. Whenever one animal encountered another, there would be antagonistic squeaks and posturings, even boxing with the forefeet. But in the wild, Clough never observed actual biting. If, however, he placed two lemmings together in a small cage, they would fight savagely until one of them died, always within twenty-four hours.

There have been many laboratory studies of the effects of crowding on animals. Overcrowding results in a slowed rate of growth and in undersized and weak adults — easily enough explained in terms of food shortage. But even when provision is made so that an abundance of food is always available, there may be striking changes in behavior and physiology. Most of the studies have been made with rodents, and in these animals the overstimulation under crowded conditions results in a disruption of the usual endocrine balance — causing, most notably, an enlargement of the adrenal cortex. The consequences are diminished reproductive functioning in both males and females, inhibition of growth, increased susceptibility to disease, and so forth. The endocrine changes under caged conditions are clear; whether comparable changes occur under crowded conditions in the wild is not so well established, though it would seem a likely explanation of abnormal behavior.

Interestingly enough, it has recently been discovered that

hormone changes are associated with the shift from solitary to migratory phase in locusts. The glands concerned are very different, of course, from the endocrine glands of mammals; but the principle of chemical control over behavior may well be the same.

Probably the best-known studies of the behavior of mammal populations under confinement are those carried out by John Calhoun with the Norway rat. He has published many papers on these studies, but perhaps the most convenient summary is that given in the February 1962 issue of *Scientific American,* entitled "Population Density and Social Pathology."

Calhoun has observed his rats in Baltimore back yards, in large outdoor enclosures, and in carefully designed laboratory cages. He has tried to make caged conditions as "natural" as possible by using large enclosures provided with nest boxes, hiding places, runways and the like. There always remains, however, the problem of evaluating the behavior of animals kept in enclosures: immigration and emigration are ruled out; one animal chased by another cannot flee from the experiment. Observations made under experimental conditions must always be checked with studies in the field if they are to be correctly interpreted. Fighting behavior in particular is apt to be exaggerated under caged conditions — witness the difference between wild and caged lemmings observed by Garrett Clough. On the other hand, it is often difficult to understand behavior in the wild without testing animals under controlled conditions. Calhoun is certainly very much aware of all of this;

yet his work has been criticized as not making sufficient allowance for the effects of restricted space.

In general Calhoun and others have found that under crowded conditions, but with ample food available, behavioral changes occur that greatly reduce reproduction. The most striking cases involve the formation of what Calhoun has called "behavioral sinks." In experiments in which a large enclosure is subdivided into pens with restricted access, dominant males may establish more or less normal reproductive relations in some pens, while the other pens will be occupied by the outcasts, who show various abnormal behavioral patterns — who show "social pathology."

Females in a behavioral sink become sloppy nest-builders or fail to make nests at all; litters are aborted or young neglected, making for a very high infant mortality. Some males become extremely phlegmatic, losing all interest in sex or in fighting. Others become hyperactive — the "probers" — attempting to mate with other males or with females not in estrus, showing what Calhoun has called "pansexual behavior." They also tend to be cannibalistic, eating the abandoned young.

Thus the "vice and misery" of the Malthusian propositions develop in rat populations as well as in human. Whether rats in nature form behavioral sinks is a matter of debate: the lemmings at least show that odd behavior may be the consequence of crowding in the wild. Inevitably one compares rats in a behavioral sink with humans in a crowded ghetto. Certainly people often behave very much like rats — as Konrad Lorenz pointed out in *On Aggression* — but I think the differences outweigh the similarities. We may, however, be able to learn something about ourselves by studying rats.

CROWDED PEOPLE

13

So MUCH FOR ANIMALS. WHAT ABOUT people? There is plenty of chance for observation of crowding — and the opportunities for study are increasing steadily. The usual present estimate for the population of the world is three and a half billion persons, and the numbers are now increasing at a rate of 2 per cent a year. This means an annual increase of 70 million: the equivalent of a new Chicago metropolitan area every month. Whatever one thinks of Chicago, this seems a little excessive.

Further, there is a tendency almost everywhere for these growing numbers of people to aggregate more and more in cities. This is true of Asia and Africa as well as of industrialized Europe and North America. If the 200 million people of the United States were scattered evenly over the landscape, the density would be 50 persons per square mile. But 70 per cent of this population lives in urban areas. New York City proper has a density of 25,000 per-

sons per square mile — 90,000 per square mile on Manhattan
Island. Lewis Herber in his book *Crisis in Our Cities* cal-
culates that in the residential parts of Manhattan the actual
density is 380,000 people per square mile — 136 individuals
for every 100-by-100-foot lot. This is achieved, of course,
by stacking the residential units.

Here surely are appropriate conditions for the formation of "behavioral sinks," and the rioting and violence of
the ghettos would seem to demonstrate that people and
rats do act much alike. I doubt, however, that the miseries
of the ghetto are purely a consequence of crowding. After
all, thousands of men can be crowded on a battleship with
no obvious damage to behavior; and conditions in a submarine are even more restrictive. To be sure, the men on
the submarine are carefully selected for personality traits;
and the situation might be very different if the crowded
ships included families instead of just men.

There are few detailed studies of the psychological effects
of crowding on people. The most thorough and best known
is a three-volume report on an intensive study of the inhabitants of midtown Manhattan by a team of social
scientists, entitled *Mental Health in the Metropolis*. The
area covered did not include ghettos, though conditions
did range from near-slum to luxury apartments. Only 18.5
per cent of the 1,660 people interviewed were found to be
free of all but inconsequential symptoms of mental illness.
All of the rest had some kind of neurotic or psychotic
symptoms, though only 2.7 per cent were incapacitated. No
hospitalized people were included in the sample. However,

a survey of the hospitals and clinics in the region showed that on an average day eight individuals per thousand were receiving outpatient psychiatric care, and five per thousand were hospitalized. None of this sounds very healthy.

It is difficult to measure mental health, because there are so many differences of opinion among psychiatrists and clinical psychologists. Physical health is easier to measure and compare, and here there is no question about the relatively greater risk to health from living in the city, despite the greater availability of medical services there. Lewis Herber in the book I mentioned above has reviewed a number of studies. Peptic ulcers and coronary attacks are understandably more common in the city, and probably have psychosomatic aspects. Lung cancer among nonsmokers is eleven times more common in an urban environment than in a rural one — smokers on the other hand have about the same rate in both environments. Lung cancer can be explained by air pollution; but, curiously, most kinds of cancer are more common in the city than in the country, which makes one wonder whether some element of stress is involved.

Reading about urban conditions, one begins to wonder why anyone lives in cities. There is, of course, a tremendous out-migration to the suburbs by people who can afford it; but this is more than balanced numerically by the in-migration from villages, towns and countryside. These are mostly people at poverty level coming to the city because that is where the jobs are, now that agriculture has become so completely mechanized. Often there are no jobs, or only jobs with inadequate pay: the resulting poverty leads to the deterioration of the inner city that has lately been causing so much concern.

We have a national conviction that the city is a poor place to raise children. In the midtown Manhattan study, residents were asked, "For growing children, do you think it is better to be brought up on a farm, in a small town, in a small city, or in a big city like New York?" In reply, only 15 per cent preferred a big city like New York. Interestingly enough, native New Yorkers disapproved of their city as an environment for children just as much as parents who had come in from outside. When asked the same question with regard to themselves, about half thought they would be better off away from New York. Yet millions of people continue to live in New York — and to raise families there.

The middle-class parents of midtown Manhattan tend to restrict the size of the family — a large proportion of the couples having only one child or none. In the slums, on the other hand, breeding seems to be unrestricted. In the racist climate that prevails in the United States, Negroes may even resent birth-control propaganda as aimed at restricting their numbers discriminatorily. Urban middle-class couples are thoroughly caught in the rat race of working their way up in the social and economic systems, so that children become a handicap; while many of the slum inhabitants have given up. Perhaps the competitive struggle, rather than the crowding, accounts for the poor mental health of the urban white-collar workers. In the case of the slums, the deprived environment can be used to explain practically anything — including mass hysteria.

I have been writing mostly about the dismal aspects of the crowded city, yet all through history cities have been the habitat of civilized man, the source of progress in the arts and sciences as well as in industry and commerce. There is something exhilarating about life in a great city, some spirit that compensates for the trials of crowding. Besides, people like crowds — most people go where other people are, packing beaches, parks, theaters, sidewalks.

The great value of the city lies in its diversity: all kinds of people with all kinds of facilities for filling their varying needs. The very concentration of people provides audiences for the theater, visitors for museums and galleries, readers for books and periodicals, and a market for an immense variety of shops. In the small town, where everyone knows all about everyone else, the pressures for conformity are great. The eccentric, the deviant, the talented move to the city where they can find more of their own kind. The city is a haven for the artist as well as for the thief.

Cities became possible back about 3000 B.C. with the discovery of methods of transporting and storing foodstuffs, so that an agricultural surplus produced by the farmers could be used to support other kinds of people — priests, kings, soldiers, smiths, philosophers. The proliferation of occupational niches in the city has continued all through history — and is going on in our own day at an accelerating rate. I suspect that this multiplicity of niches is what enables people to survive under crowded conditions — conditions that rats could not tolerate. After all, rats lack the means of avoiding the stress of very frequent contact between individuals that occupational diversity provides.

This is the argument of the Chicago sociologist Nathan Keyfitz in an article in the issue of *BioScience* for December 1966. "If the city is, on the one side, a jungle of potentially infinite and destroying competition, on the other it shows a nearly infinite capacity of its members to differentiate themselves, to become useful to one another, to become needed."

In psychological jargon, the niche gives a feeling of identity. We are engineers, teachers, cabdrivers, physicians or what have you. We thus belong to a group; but within each group there are numerous subgroups reflecting the specialized knowledge or skill of each of us. There may be a hundred specialties within such a field as electronic engineering, as Keyfitz points out — the possible specializations within a modern city are truly almost infinite. Also, there are almost endless organizations within the city, sometimes competing, as with banks or stores, sometimes providing general service, as with the educational or telephone systems. These organizations further pattern space in the city, serve also to reduce stressful contacts among individuals.

The man in the city comes in contact with hundreds of other people every day, but most of these contacts, unlike those among crowded rats, are not stressful. We are not involved in the private life of the cabdriver, the bank clerk or the reporter for *The New York Times*. We usually know little about our physician or lawyer beyond confidence in his professional skill. As we move between the small world of home and the small world of the office or business place, we pass many hundreds of people, but for the most part this results in no meaningful relationships. We are inured to other people.

This kind of individual support is generally lacking in the ghetto — which is probably one of the causes of ghetto unrest. The unemployed or the underemployed person becomes Ralph Ellison's "invisible man," uncertain about work, not knowing how to get money for rent or groceries or the installment on the television set. Ghetto life has been graphically described in the Kerner report on riots, and in books like the novels of James Baldwin and the reports on the life of Puerto Ricans and Mexicans by Oscar Lewis. Prostitution, alcoholism, drug addiction, violence become rife. The Kerner report found that 42 per cent of the Negro families with incomes of under $3,000 had no father living at home. The ghetto world is in large part a matriarchy — with mother constantly distracted by the problems of survival. The ghetto thus comes to resemble the behavioral sink of Calhoun's rats, except that it continues to reproduce.

Poverty tends to shackle us, and wealth to free us, without much relation to the intensity of crowdedness. This makes me wonder about that "territorial imperative" of Robert Ardrey and others. If the human species is strongly territorial, how did the formation of cities ever get started? I share with Ardrey, Lorenz and others the feeling that Old Stone Age man lived in social groups with individuals within the group forming a dominance hierarchy or peck order, and with the whole group occupying a defended territory. But I suspect that with the beginning of settled life and agriculture during the Neolithic, territoriality started to break down. Cities, city-states and empires — with their wars and rebellions — represent cultural ideas rather than territorial instinct.

The "turfs" of the gangs of adolescent hoodlums are the nearest thing to territories in a modern city. I can think of no way of determining whether these represent the arousal of some latent instinct in these youth, or whether they are a secondary development, only analogous to the territories of wild animals. Jane Jacobs, in her thought-provoking book *The Death and Life of Great American Cities*, discusses the extension of the turf idea to exclusive residential areas where no strangers are wanted. This surely is cultural rather than instinctive — as, I think, are all forms of discrimination.

To explain discrimination in terms of peck order seems to me as far-fetched as to explain war in terms of territoriality. Some vague leftover of inborn aggression may be found in the one, and of dominance in the other, but they are well buried under accumulated ideas. The peck-order pattern that emerges in prisons, schools and adolescent gangs may well have an instinctive basis; but this dominance among a group of individuals seems to me different from mass discrimination against Negroes, Jews, Protestants, Indians or whomever.

Dominance hierarchy in our society is largely formal: rank in the armed forces, chain of command in business, position within the university and the like. Whether the drive to become a general in the army is comparable with the drive of a gorilla to become the Old Man of the tribe, I don't know. But in both cases the structuring serves to promote the stability of the group.

The human animal clearly can be crowded into quite dense aggregations without obvious immediate physical or mental deterioration (possible long-term effects are something else) — if there are ample resources for support. I tend to think this is partly due to the weakness of our territorial drive and the formality of our systems of dominance hierarchy. This is comforting when one looks at those multiplying billions in the years ahead — except that there is always the catch about resources. The vice and misery of the Malthusian propositions will not necessarily persist if we can find food, housing and some amenities for all of mankind. But it takes considerable optimism to think this possible. Under present conditions crowded people are apt to be miserable people who sometimes act in as bizarre a fashion as Calhoun's rats. The plea of the Kerner report that we must do something about the ghettos in our cities is surely valid if we wish to have a healthy nation.

AGGRESSION

14

AGGRESSION HAS BECOME A COMMON WORD these days. It has, of course, long been thrown about in discussions of international politics; and clinical psychologists tend to find aggressive impulses in everyone, however meek he may seem. But the word has escaped from politics and psychology into general discussion, largely because of a series of widely read books, especially Konrad Lorenz, *On Aggression;* Robert Ardrey, *The Territorial Imperative;* and Desmond Morris, *The Naked Ape.* One which I found most thought-provoking of all in relation to man's problems — *Human Aggression,* by the British psychiatrist Anthony Storr — seems to have received much less attention from the general public.

The reactions to these books have varied from enthusiasm to downright hostility, with literary figures tending toward enthusiasm, and scientists showing a whole spectrum of reactions — depending I suppose on the particular set of ideas to which they are committed. Anthropologists and psychologists have generally been hostile. M. F. Ashley Montagu, the well-known anthropologist, went so far as to collect a series of critical reviews of the Lorenz and Ardrey books which he published under the title *Man and Aggression,* hoping "to put the record straight, to correct what threatens to become an epidemic error concerning the causes of man's aggression, and to redirect attention to a consideration of the real causes of such behavior."

The bitterness of some of the attacks puzzles me. Ardrey, of course, is an intruder: a former dramatist who has now taken to writing about animals and human behavior, where he is seen to have no business. Lorenz, undeniably an eminent scientist and one of the founders of the type of behavior study labeled "ethology," gets somewhat more respectful treatment — though the error of his ways is plain to many of his colleagues. I suspect that most of his fellow zoologists think that Desmond Morris simply found an easy way to make money by writing a popular book with lots of sex in it — which is, after all, pretty reprehensible. Scientists are not nearly so impersonal and impartial as they like to make out — indeed, they are people, and they can be quite aggressive when their particular intellectual territories are invaded.

Lorenz and Ardrey have both oversimplified, and have overstressed certain aspects of animal behavior in the effort to make their points — each more or less admits this in the course of his book. But for some reason this seems to be necessary to make people listen. The late Rachel Carson did the same thing, on a quite different subject, in *Silent Spring* — to the indignation of the pesticide manufacturers. But she succeeded in arousing a public awareness which I think is entirely to the good.

The objectives of Lorenz and Ardrey seem to me valid: to bring the discussion of human nature out into the open, and to try to look at the biological inheritance that is surely still with us. The clinical psychologists have had too much of a monopoly on this for a long time, probably because they are the most verbal of the scientists concerned. Or maybe because they are the most aggressive.

I greatly admire the work of Lorenz, Tinbergen and some of the other people who call themselves "ethologists" (why did they have to invent such a word — why not just study animal behavior?). Sometimes, as an outsider, I think the differences among the various schools of psychological thought are more a matter of words than of ideas — but then words seem to be the cause of a great deal of human misunderstanding.

As for Robert Ardrey — I think he makes his own best defense. The human condition is a matter of concern for all of us, and we had all better think about it, talk about it, and — if we can write — air our opinions. I am astonished at Ardrey's mastery of the relevant biological literature. I don't think anyone can quarrel with the animal-reporting in either book, except for a tendency to minimize behavior that doesn't fit the thesis. The difficulties start when we turn from other animals to the behavior of people.

As I remarked earlier, our anatomy and physiology is

not much different from that of other mammals, except for our much-touted big brain. (Desmond Morris notes that man also has the biggest penis of all the primates — but the psychologists haven't stressed this.) If anatomy and physiology have persisted through the course of evolution from protohominid to hominid, presumably behavioral characteristics have persisted also. But they have become deeply buried by the tremendously increased importance of teaching and learning ("extrasomatic inheritance"), which result in what the anthropologists call culture. Digging through this cultural overlay to the biological animal underneath has so far met with almost total defeat. But if we are to gain any understanding of ourselves, we must keep on trying — and I salute Lorenz and Ardrey for their attempts.

On Aggression seemed to me misleading as a title for the Lorenz book. I am told that he chose it himself and carefully checked the English version, so that Marjorie Wilson, the translator, cannot be blamed for the terminology. The German title is *Das sogenannte Böse.* I don't think there is any close English equivalent for *Böse* — it is a sort of blend of anger, maliciousness, evil. But the "so-called" gives a much-needed biological perspective; though I must admit that "So-called Maliciousness" and even "So-called Aggression" would make lousy book titles.

The living world of our planet forms an ongoing system which has been working on the same principles for some hundreds of millions of years now. Life as we know it comes in packages which we call "individuals," and the packages are of many different kinds, "species." The system includes mechanisms for such things as the transference of energy and the cycling of materials, for the diversification and development of species — and also for the distribution, spacing and maintenance of interrelationships among the packages. Some relationships we call antagonistic, some cooperative; but to my mind this reflects, not the way nature works, but the way we think. Lorenz has dedicated himself, in his book, to showing the adaptive value of one kind of interrelationship among individuals of the same species — one of the relationships that we call antagonistic, that we see as aggressive behavior on the part of one individual to another. The trouble is that when we call this "aggression" we think of it as bad; but if such behavior promotes the survival of the species — and much of Lorenz's book is devoted to showing this — adjectives like "bad" and "good" become irrelevant.

It is another matter when we turn to *Homo sapiens*. Our peculiarity is that we frequently kill one another as a result of our antagonisms — something that is rare and accidental in nature, though common enough when animals are confined in cages. Lorenz points out that ordinarily, in the course of biological evolution, inhibiting behavior develops along with dangerous weapons like teeth and claws. In the rapid course of human cultural change, weapons have outpaced behavioral controls. But if there is any simple biological impulse underlying aggressive behavior in man, it has got warped into a tremendous variety of · shapes during our cultural history.

I have come to think that "aggression," when used with reference to man, is a sort of wastebasket word into which we have dumped all sorts of garbage. What kind of shared animal behavior could explain one drunk slugging another in a bar, a man impersonally pulling a lever to demolish a city, a thief knifing his victim in the back, the burning of a heretic, the massacre of Syrians, Indians, Christians or Jews? These things are the consequences of cultural attitudes. If there is, behind all of this, some animal impulse gone berserk, it has proliferated into an amazingly wide range of forms.

I agree with Lorenz that it would be a great help if we could learn to take ourselves less seriously. But I am not sure that either of us knows how to accomplish this. I know I don't. I keep trying, but it is difficult in the face of the headlines in the daily paper.

Curiously, I have also recently come to think that the word "territory" as used by biologists may cover a variety of quite different things. I say "curiously" because I have been writing about it, lecturing about it, observing it for years without any qualms. It seems simple: an area defended by an individual or group against intrusion by other individuals of the same species. If an animal stays in the same region, but does not defend against intrusion, the area is called a "home range."

The idea of territory first gained general currency as a consequence of a little book called *Territory in Bird Life,* published in 1920 by an amateur British ornithologist, Eliot Howard. Territorial behavior since then has been studied intensively by many people, observing many kinds of animals in different parts of the world. The ornithologist Margaret Nice, in an article published in the *American Midland Naturalist* in 1941, distinguished six kinds of territory among birds: mating, nesting and feeding ground; mating and nesting area but not the whole feeding ground; mating station only; immediate surroundings of nest only; winter territories; and roosting points. Are these all the consequence of some single basic drive?

Take mating territories, for instance — called "leks" in the case of the European grouse. In this case males of a given bird species will assemble when sexually active, each male maintaining a separate "territory" near or even contiguous to that of the others, in which he dances or displays in some way. Females, attracted by the commotion, pick the male with which they will mate — goodness knows on what basis. This kind of behavior is known in birds of some eleven different families, so that it has presumably evolved independently several different times.

Among the birds showing this behavior are the Neotropical manakins. I have a pair of Costa Rican blue-backed manakins (*Chiroxiphia linearis*) in my greenhouse — the male named Scrooge because he looked so ratty when he arrived in juvenile plumage; the female thus logically became Scrounge. I was dubious about introducing a male manakin for fear he might tear up plants in the course of making a dance arena. But he didn't. When feeling sexy, he dances back and forth from the rim of one flowerpot to another, making a curious snarl-like cry, very different from his ordinary call. He gets quite frantic, but Scrounge never pays any attention. I wonder whether several competing males are necessary to arouse the female. I want to test this if I ever manage to get more manakins.

Is this territorial defense of a dancing arena a manifestation of the same basic drive as a hummingbird defending a feeding tube? Or a band of howler monkeys defending their patch of forest from intrusion by other bands?

The situation among our relatives, the primates, is particularly puzzling: which is no help when one tries to decide whether there is any basic territorial drive left in the human animal. Gibbon families are strictly territorial. George Schaller (*The Mountain Gorilla*) found that a gorilla band tended to stay in a particular home range, but did not defend this from intrusion by other bands — though when two bands happened to be close together, there was no friendly interchange. Chimpanzees, as far as I can judge from recent studies (all of this field work has been beautifully summarized in a book edited by Irven DeVore, *Primate Behavior*) are best described as miscellaneous, with shifting patterns of social behavior that hardly involve either aggression or territoriality.

As for conflict behavior itself: among gorillas it takes the form of staring. Schaller observed, for instance, a conflict between two adult males of different groups that had happened to come together. One male walked rapidly toward the other, "and the two stared into each other's eyes, their faces a foot apart. These giants of the forest, each with the strength of several men, were settling their differences, whatever they were, not by fighting but rather by trying to stare each other down." And those aggressive howler monkeys of Panama defend their territories by roaring at one another. Staring and yelling persist in us as forms of aggressive behavior — if that were all, there would be no problem.

As for those protohominids, one would have to have a time machine to go back and find out about their behavior. I suspect Lorenz, Ardrey, Morris and the others are right: that our ancestors lived in small hunting bands which roamed over defended territories, and that some trace of this territoriality lingers in our present behavioral makeup. As I mentioned in the discussion of "Eating and Being Eaten," there is evidence that our ancestors were predators or hunters for a long time. Our contemporary cousins among the apes are either vegetarian (gorillas) or general scroungers on fruits and easily caught small animals (chimpanzees). With mammals it seems to me that territorial defense is more apt to develop among predators than among vegetarians, and that probably the protohominids behaved more like wolves than like gorillas. But even if we still have territorial tendencies, this doesn't mean that we have to kill one another when we disagree. The force of culture, of learned behavior, is so great that it can overcome any innate tendency.

Among the reactions to the aggression books, I particularly liked an article by the British anthropologist Geoffrey Gorer entitled "Man Has No 'Killer' Instinct," published in *The New York Times Magazine* for November 27, 1966 (and reprinted by Ashley Montagu in his anthology). Gorer points out that there are "a few societies where men seem to find no pleasure in dominating over, hurting or killing the members of other societies." He cites the Arapesh of New Guinea, the Lepchas of Sikkim and the pygmies of the Congo. "These societies are, of course, small, weak, technologically backward, and living in inaccessible country; only so could they survive the power-seeking of their uninhibited neighbors."

"What seem to me the most significant common traits in these peaceful societies," he notes, "are that they all manifest enormous gusto for concrete physical pleasures — eating, drinking, sex, laughter — and that they all make very little distinction between the ideal characters of men and women, particularly that they have no ideal of brave, aggressive masculinity."

I wish I had thought of that. Books like Claude Brown's *Manchild in the Promised Land,* about growing up in Harlem — where both masculinity and aggression are rampant — make a neat demonstration of Gorer's thesis. At the other extreme, maybe our hope for the future lies with the hippies, who have adopted all the characteristics of the non-aggressive societies, including the failure to distinguish sharply in dress and role between the sexes. The hippies certainly can be obstinate — to the distress of their elders — but I see no signs of aggression, at least when they are left alone.

ALIENS IN THE LANDSCAPE

15

$\mathbf{F}$OR THE LAST SEVERAL CHAPTERS I HAVE been writing about various aspects of the human ecosystem: relations between humans and other animals, food, crud production, crowding, the aggressive tendencies that make the system so turbulent. Another human characteristic is the desire to move animals and plants around the world — which has resulted in man's becoming a major factor in the geographical distribution of a large number of kinds of organisms.

Look at those starlings. I haven't come across anyone who could be called a friend of the starlings. In the case of pigeons people can be divided into pro- and anti- factions (with janitors solidly antipigeon), but the prostarling group is either completely absent or very quiet. A great deal of ingenuity has gone into the problem of discouraging starlings: gunfire and other noises, electric shock, playing recordings of starling alarm calls and most recently a never-drying sticky substance, which seems to work because the birds don't like to get their feet gummed up.

Yet in the last century quite a number of people thought it would be nice to have starlings in this country, and several attempts were made to get them established — unsuccessful until 1890, when about eighty pairs were released in Central Park. The first starlings to breed here may well have done so under the eaves of the American Museum of Natural History — though the museum cannot be blamed for the introduction. The effort to establish starlings is the more puzzling because the birds had already proved to be pests when introduced into New Zealand and Australia, and they had never been admired by British farmers. But people set on bringing in some new species of plant or animal are not easily discouraged. Man has been influencing biogeography for quite a while now.

Of course many introductions are accidental rather than purposeful. Microbes, insects and weed seeds are particularly apt to accompany man on his travels as members of the human entourage. Among mammals, rats and mice have done quite well, and a number of lizards have got widely spread around the tropics by hitchhiking on ships. The uninvited travelers are apt to be pests — about half of the major insect pests of crops in the United States are aliens, accidentally introduced — and this has led to the institution of quarantines to prevent the entry of unwanted organisms.

"Quarantine" comes from the Italian *quaranta,* referring to the forty-day period of isolation imposed on a ship — cargo, passengers and crew — if there were indications of unusual disease. The practice is said to have started in fourteenth-century Venice, long before there was any scientific basis for the action. Since Pasteur and the acceptance of the germ theory of disease, quarantines have been elaborated and systematized, but in many cases it is still possible to debate whether the restrictions are worth all the trouble they cause.

We are particularly sensitive about introducing new insects, as anyone knows who has tried to carry fruit or plants across a frontier. I am still not sure whether such quarantine barriers are effective enough to warrant the inconvenience — a doubt that I inherited from my father-in-law, David Fairchild. He was head of the Office of Seed and Plant Introduction of the Department of Agriculture for many years, and dedicated his life to moving possibly useful or ornamental plants around the globe. His good friend (as my wife mentions in Chapter 4) was Charles Marlatt, chief of the Bureau of Entomology. The friendship was badly strained when Marlatt established the insect quarantine — and spoiled many of Fairchild's plants by fumigating them.

Fairchild argued that the quarantine was useless because it would not be possible to carry out an inspection thorough enough to eliminate all potential pests. He once sought to prove his point at the border of California — a state that is particularly careful about alien insects and the foodstuffs on which they are likely to travel — by insisting that if they were going to inspect the car before permitting it to enter California, they should be thorough about it. He got the inspectors to drag out all the suitcases and open them and go through the automobile carefully as tempers became strained and traffic accumulated on the road behind. He drove on, feeling smug about the whole affair. Presently his wife reached into the pocket on the car door to get a handkerchief — and pulled out an orange!

The various plant-quarantine services usually publish statistics on the number of thousands of insects that are intercepted every year. There are, of course, no figures on the number that they fail to find, and some major pests have become established despite quarantine. The Dutch elm disease is a case, though this is complicated since both native and foreign bark beetles and a fungus are involved. The fungus, according to Charles Elton in his book *The Ecology of Invasions,* was first identified in Ohio in 1930 and is thought to have entered with infected elm timber used for veneers. Elton discusses several other pests that have been introduced "in spite of heavy screens of quarantine."

That alien species are not easily established in new country is shown by the history of attempts at deliberate introduction. There were at least five or six efforts to establish those starlings in the United States before the success of 1890. Goodness knows how many attempts have been made to establish other birds in this country: among them are several species of thrushes, finches and titmice, the nightingale, woodlark, British robin and mute swan. At one time it looked as though the European goldfinch and skylark had become established, but they died out.

Only six wild species of alien birds can be called successful: the Hungarian partridge, the ring-necked pheasant, the starling, the house sparrow, the European tree sparrow (in Missouri) and the Chinese spotted dove (in the vicinity of Los Angeles). (I regard pigeons as escaped cultigens.)

Europeans living in New Zealand and Hawaii have been particularly addicted to introducing birds and mammals for reasons of sentiment or sport. One would think it would be relatively easy to establish aliens in these islands — especially since both regions had rather limited bird faunas and no mammals except bats. But G. M. Thompson, in his book *The Naturalization of Animals and Plants in New Zealand,* reported that of 130 attempts to introduce bird species only 24 succeeded. George Munro, in *Birds of Hawaii,* reports efforts to introduce 96 species, of which 19 have become well established, while 12 more seem likely to succeed.

There is considerable discussion as to whether the alien birds in Hawaii constitute a threat to the native perching birds — the peculiar thrushes and honeycreepers. Certainly the native birds are in a bad way: Munro estimates that 25 species have a fair chance of survival, while 30 others are either already extinct or likely to become so. Hawaii, however, illustrates a general phenomenon: that aliens are apt to be most abundant in the man-altered landscape. This is probably because birds that are easily established are kinds that get along well with man — witness those starlings. Extinction of many local animals in all parts of the world is apt to be the consequence of multiplying human numbers, of man's activity in clearing and culti-vating land, destroying the natural habitats. The survivors, except for the inhabitants of nature reserves, are apt to be what I have called the opportunists — the species that thrive in the human ecosystem.

I first became aware of this peculiarity of our associates some years ago when I got into a part of the upper Orinoco drainage in South America where man had had no detect-able role in altering the landscape. The plants and animals I had thought of as common — weeds, roadside birds and butterflies — disappeared or were found only in such natural open habitats as river sandbars. The organisms associated with civilized or agricultural man are a very special lot. One theory is that many of them were saved from extinction by man's coming along just in time, that they would not have survived in undisturbed biological communities. Those animals and plants around us that look so tough are really the weaklings of the biosphere.

I suspect, then, that the extraordinary Hawaiian family of honeycreepers would be disappearing at just about the same rate if man had never brought any alien birds to the islands. On the other hand, if man should disappear from these islands, most of his associates might disappear too. Unfortunately, "most" is not "all." Quite a few of the man-moved aliens in various parts of the world would undoubtedly get along very well without him, to the detriment of the native biota.

It is interesting that many of the fresh-water fishes that man has moved thrive in environments that appear un-

altered by human action. This is particularly true of such
predatory species as the brown trout, the rainbow trout
and the large-mouthed black bass. In many places where
these were introduced there were no native competitors —
the case, for instance, in New Zealand, Tasmania and isolated mountain lakes in many parts of the world — so that
the success of the introduction is understandable. The
trout, however, have also flourished in lakes where the
local fauna seemed complete and well balanced. This is
true in the South American Lake Titicaca, where rainbow
trout have almost eliminated the indigenous fishes. This
might be justified from the narrow human point of view
if rainbow trout were considered better food; but in the
case of Lake Titicaca the local people preferred their own
fishes, and a thriving industry has been destroyed for the
benefit of a few sportsmen.

The success of fishes is not limited to these larger
predators — look at the teeming carp in many lakes and
streams in the United States. The small topminnow of our
southeastern states, *Gambusia affinis,* has been spread widely
over the world in attempts to control malaria, since the
fish has an insatiable appetite for mosquito larvae. It now
teems in the marshes and ponds of southern Europe, North
Africa, South Africa, Southeast Asia and parts of South
America. I don't believe *Gambusia* has ever been very
effective in controlling malaria — the fish does not readily
penetrate water thickly matted with aquatic plants, where
the mosquito larvae thrive. On the other hand, the *Gambusia* has had a disastrous effect on other fishes in waters

where it has been introduced — presumably being respon-sible for the extinction of a number of interesting species in various parts of the world.

Other exceptions to the rule that man-moved aliens thrive best in man-altered landscapes are found among mammals, especially where these have been introduced into oceanic islands with few or no native species. The success of the mongoose in the West Indies and Hawaii is a fine example.

A Jamaican planter, W. Bancroft Espeut, imported four pairs of mongoose from Calcutta in 1872 for the purpose of controlling the rats which were causing great damage to the cane fields. The introduction was an immediate success, leading other cane-growing islands to try the exper-iment. But the success was short-lived; after a few years the rats in the cane fields became as abundant as ever. The rats, it seemed, had learned to nest high off the ground where the mongoose couldn't reach them. The mongoose then took to catching chickens and a wide variety of ground-living vertebrates — frogs, lizards, birds, small mammals. The mongoose itself came to be universally regarded as a pest.

Should we stop this practice of moving plants and animals around the world? The disasters have not convinced many wildlife officials. Sportsmen in the United States are still enthusiastically supporting the importation of game, and gardeners are not likely to stop trying new plants. The temptation is particularly great to try establishing the varied animals of the African grasslands in the southwestern

United States and on the plains of Argentina. The case against moving animals around has been ably stated by George Laycock in *The Alien Animals,* which also has an excellent bibliography on the subject of animal introductions. I think Laycock is right; but I also suspect that there is no chance that we will abandon this particular method of altering the landscapes in which we live. We should, at least, learn to be more careful than we have been in the past.

SKIN-OUT BIOLOGY

16

IF WE ARE TO LEARN TO BE MORE CAREFUL in our treatment of various aspects of the biosphere, we need more emphasis on the natural-history side of biology in our schools. Biology has very generally become a required subject in high school, usually at the sophomore level. Most colleges have adopted the principle of "distribution," meaning that every student should be exposed to a number of courses in the natural sciences, social sciences and humanities, and must at least have a certain level of skill in mathematics and some foreign language. The idea is to develop broadly educated citizens by acquainting them with a variety of different kinds of knowledge. This mostly involves taking introductory courses. I like to make the quip that introductory courses are designed for the purpose of discouraging interest in the particular subject — and that they are generally successful. The trouble, of course, is that the instructors are apt to be most interested in the minority

157

of students who will possibly be future specialists in the fields in question. The others are supposed to acquire understanding through some obscure process of contagion; the rate of infection, however, is not very high.

The situation in biology seems to me particularly dismal — an opinion that is shared by a large number of my colleagues, though we are far from agreement on what should be done about it. One difficulty is a basic split among biologists themselves on the matter of where emphasis should be placed in teaching. The eminent paleontologist George Gaylord Simpson has discussed this in an issue of *The American Scholar* for Summer 1967 under the title "The Crisis in Biology." Simpson distinguishes between "molecular" and "organismal" biology: between the scientists interested in the physics and chemistry of living processes, and those interested in the workings of the organisms themselves.

This distinction is probably more logical than the one I have long made between the "skin-in" and "skin-out" aspects of biology. I meant to separate the study of the whole animal or plant — its behavior, its place in the biological community and in the evolutionary scheme — from the study of the ways the different parts inside work. The anatomist or physiologist may still be interested in seeing how the parts go together to make the whole organism; but the molecular biologists often seem to lose sight of the whole organism in their pursuit of chemical details.

The physico-chemical point of view toward life has a long history, but it is currently particularly fashionable because of a series of undeniably important discoveries. The most notable and talked-about of these concern the determination of the structures of the nucleic acids DNA and RNA, which seem to lie at the basis of heredity. But there is still much to learn. Simpson quotes "one of the stormy petrels of biology" as saying "that DNA is the 'secret of life' is less true . . . than that life is the secret of DNA."

Teachers and textbook writers understandably want to reflect the most recent developments in their subject, and this means, as Simpson remarks, that ". . . biology students may be taught recent and esoteric bits of biochemistry but not the systematics, physiology and ecology of organisms." Plants and animals are still with us, however; and it seems to me that the most important thing that the ordinary student should get from biology is some understanding of the forms of life with which we share the planet, and their relationships among themselves and with our species. I don't worry about the future specialist, because in the long run he will have to educate himself — the teacher's problem in this case is to encourage him, and to be available and helpful in whatever way he can.

I like to distinguish between training in particular skills and techniques, and education, which I take to be concerned with ideas and understandings. Education in this sense should help us to cope with our own problems, and with the problems of our society and of mankind as a whole. The great problems that face mankind, as I see them, are the population explosion; the threat — and reality — of war; the conservation or wise management of resources;

and the maintenance of a healthy environment. None of these can be considered purely biological: since the concern is with people, the whole range of the social sciences is involved. But the human species has evolved from an animal background and forms, inescapably, a part of the earth's biosphere, so that biological concepts and facts are also relevant and important. Yet the pertinent parts of biology, of natural history — ecology, behavior, systematics, even evolutionary theory — get very little attention in our textbooks.

At the University of Michigan I try to meet this problem with a course called "Zoology in Human Affairs" (the title was not my idea, but it leaves me free to talk about almost anything). Enrolment is limited to juniors and seniors who are not science majors. I can thus presume some previous experience with such subjects as psychology, anthropology, sociology, economics and the like. To preserve my own sanity, I try to make the course somewhat different each year. But I also try always to cover to some extent such topics as the organization and interrelatedness of biological communities (including the man-altered landscape); the dynamics of animal populations, emphasizing the peculiarities of the present human situation; the history of ideas about evolution and man's place in nature; the epidemiology (natural history) of disease, chiefly because it has been my own special research interest; and animal behavior with emphasis on aspects that may be relevant to our own evolution and development.

After a couple of experiments, I have abandoned the

idea of using a textbook. I want the students to find that reading about biology can be interesting as well as instructive, so I have them get a series of four or five paperback "trade books." Whether or not to use one of my own books remains an open question. At one time or another I have tried *The Nature of Natural History, The Forest and the Sea* and *Man in Nature,* but I always have a guilty conscience because I feel that the students get enough of me in listening to the lectures — and besides, it stops me from making cracks about professors who use their own books. Student reaction to such books, however, has been favorable; they tell me that they like the feeling of knowing the author while reading a book. But I still feel sheepish, and there is always the danger of saying the same thing in lecture that I have written in the book.

I have made one exception to the use of paperbacks. I want some book to give a background of the ideas of ecology, and after trying a number of the available paperbacks, I have settled, for the last three years, on Peter Farb's *Ecology* in the "Life Nature Library." Like all of the *Life* books it is beautifully illustrated, and something I hope students will want to keep. *King Solomon's Ring,* by Konrad Lorenz, is a perennial favorite. It is, as they say, "anecdotal," but I can explain the psychological theories about animal behavior in lecture. George Schaller's *The Year of the Gorilla* gives them a special case of a field study of one of the great apes, and I try to sketch the other recent studies of wild primates in lecture. One year I tried Darwin's *Voyage of the Beagle.* I hoped it would give them a glimpse of geographical diversity, some insight into the Darwin personality, and a feeling for a natural history not yet permeated by evolutionary thought. But to my surprise the students found it tedious and uninteresting.

Each year I try one or two books I have not used before. If the majority of the students find a book dull, I do not use it again, regardless of my personal opinion. I want the material to be accurate, but I also want the reader to enjoy the experience. I am trying to give the students an appreciation of the scientific enterprise through exposure to a few aspects of "organismal biology." I do not see how they can get this by memorizing the names for the appendages of the crayfish, or even by trying to master the chemical complexities of intracellular metabolism.

I like the remark made by Joseph Wood Krutch in his book *The Great Chain of Life*: "To proceed from the dissection of earthworms to the dissection of cats . . . is not necessarily to learn reverence for life or to develop any of the various kinds of 'feeling for nature' which many of the old naturalists believed was the essential thing. To expect such courses to do anything of the sort is as sensible as it would be to expect an apprenticed embalmer to emerge with a greater love and respect for his fellow man."

NATURAL HISTORY IN CITIES

17

IN THE COURSE OF MY CAMPAIGN FOR MORE emphasis on "skin-out" biology in high-school teaching, I have often been told that this is fine for country kids, but that it is not adapted to the city environment. I have to admit that it is much easier to see a wide variety of plants and animals in the country. But I do not believe that this should be the governing consideration; on the contrary, the presumed lack of familiarity would make it even more important to give city people some understanding of the biosphere. How many children are there who have never seen a cow?

As a nation we are becoming more and more urban. In 1910, according to the Bureau of the Census, 45.7 per cent of the population of the United States was urban; by 1960 the percentage in metropolitan areas had risen to 69.9, and the trend continues. City people thus form a majority of our population, and their votes will determine how we manage our portion of this spaceship earth. If we are to save any unmodified landscapes and maintain (or achieve) a healthy environment, we need the support of these city people. Most of them will be exposed to biology in high school, and this seems the logical place to arouse their interest in environmental planning, conservation of resources, combatting pollution and the like.

As a matter of fact, there are plenty of opportunities to study natural history in cities — even though cities present a rather special aspect of the subject. In high-school teaching I think it would be useful to have a greenhouse, and visits to zoos, botanic gardens and museums would be in order — important resources that are unavailable in a small town. But beyond this, an astonishing number of kinds of animals and plants have been able to adapt to the urban environment. Frank Lutz, for many years Curator of Insects at the American Museum of Natural History, published a book in 1941 on the insects he had collected in his back yard — 75 by 100 feet, and a block from the railway station in Ramsey, New Jersey. He found 1,402 species — and entitled his book *A Lot of Insects.*

A midtown apartment could not compete with Dr. Lutz's New Jersey back yard. But it might have cockroaches, silverfish, flies and spiders; and in run-down neighborhoods other animals could be added to the list. In many apartments there are aquaria with tropical fish; and a terrarium offers a way to keep lizards and frogs. One young friend of mine keeps a small boa constrictor in his room. Apartment-house horticulturists nowadays can choose from a considerable number of different shade-tolerant plants. Then there are dogs and cats, as well as canaries, finches, parrots and other pets. Thus even an urban apartment has natural-history possibilities.

The city is the extreme form of the man-altered landscape, and its inhabitants include all five of the subdivisions of the human entourage that I discussed in the chapter on "Captives and Cultigens." One might argue that all of the plant and animal residents of metropolitan areas belong to this entourage that is dependent in some way on man. There are many migrant birds — but they are not residents. Even the inconspicuous organisms of the soil must be greatly affected by human action. Animals like opossums and raccoons that rummage in suburban garbage fit very nicely, I think, into the class that I called opportunists.

Of other groups, the cultigens include the ubiquitous dogs and cats — assuming for the moment that cats can be classified as "domesticated" — as well as plants like the fancy hybrid orchids that some people are able to grow in the light from windows. Captives run the gamut of animals that can be bought in pet shops, and include quite a few wild plants like the cacti that are becoming increasingly popular. Among the inquilines are rats, mice, cockroaches and a variety of other insects.

Bedbugs, common enough in many Old World cities (do we still allow them in the United States?), present a nice problem in classification: should they be called inquilines or parasites? They live directly off man, but they don't associate with him except for feeding. My memories of bedbugs include the wicker chairs in the lobby of the tourist hotel in Salonika: in prewar days these harbored a large population of bugs which lived by nipping the arms of resting guests (or guides). I wonder whether the present Greek government has been able to cope with this problem. True parasites include lice and fleas. I don't know about the prevalence of lice in American cities, but London, when slum children were evacuated during the blitz, turned out to be well supplied.

John Kieran, in his book *Natural History of New York City*, reports that in one typical year 276,119 dogs were licensed and that in the same year the S.P.C.A. destroyed 59,413 dogs, presumably mostly strays, and 133,436 cats. Kieran does not think that this means there are more than twice as many cats as dogs in the city, because cats breed faster than dogs and kittens are more apt to be unwanted than puppies. He estimates the actual cat population of the city to be about 300,000.

Census statistics on animals in cities (other than man himself) are hard to come by. Dr. David Davis, who studied the rat population of Baltimore for many years, estimated that in 1944 the city harbored 400,000 rats (the human population at that time was 659,000). He believed that the rats declined in numbers to 165,000 in 1947 and 65,000 in 1949. Whether this downward trend has continued I don't know. Certainly rats are still common enough in many parts of our cities, as became rather obvious in New York with the strike of the garbage collectors. I was interested, in reading the Kerner report on riots, to come across the estimate that there were 14,000 cases of rat-bite in the United States in 1965, mostly in the ghettos of our cities — another mark of the miserable living conditions.

Vermin are much less abundant in American cities now than they used to be. This is partly because of the widespread use of pesticides, but it also reflects the decline of the horse in human transportation: livery stables provided a haven for rats, flies and other animals, while the manure in the streets supported hordes of English sparrows. I don't know whether it would be possible to measure the noxious side effects of horses against those of automobiles — they are so very different. Horses produced flies and smells, while automobiles pollute the atmosphere — and automobiles nowadays multiply much faster. In the United States automobiles (and trucks) take up far more physical space than the bodies of people; they still don't need as much space for residence and recreation as people — but enabling them to move is a major city problem.

Automobiles modify urban natural history by their contribution to air pollution. Smog is generally deleterious to vegetation, as every farmer in the vicinity of Los Angeles knows. Among crops, spinach, grapes and tobacco are particularly susceptible, according to the book *Poisons in the Air* by Edward Edelson and Fred Warshofsky. Of trees, conifers are especially easily damaged. The most resistant of trees in the northern urban environment are the ailanthus ("tree of heaven"), the gingko and the London plane. It is interesting that all three of these are foreign to the United States, and that the first two are from China, where they are both sacred, growing chiefly in temple grounds. What, in the past Chinese environment, would promote resistance to smog? The gingko, further, is a botanical survivor from the geological past which now is known to occur only in the man-altered landscape. Since it does not seem to be sufficiently modified to be a true cultigen, maybe it could be classed as an "obligate opportunist."

Among opportunists, weeds have long fascinated me — plants that most people dislike, pull up, cut down, spray with herbicides, they yet persist and flourish in the man-altered landscape. They seem sturdy, they manage well in gardens and lawns and vacant lots, along railway tracks and in similar improbable places. But most of them would be very rare if man did not clear land for them. In many cases, as I noted before, it seems likely that weeds are plant species that would have become extinct if man had not come along in time to save them.

I find lawns puzzling. Why are people so dead set against crabgrass and dandelions? I don't see much difference between crabgrass and lawn grass — why not let the former take over? And dandelions add nice spots of color. I have a letter from a man in Philadelphia, Joseph P. Walker, saying that "Dr. Jack McCormick and I are presently working on the question of why people mow grass. . . . What are the origins of mowers and mowing? What, if any, psychological motivation is there for mowing?" I couldn't help any with anwers, but I put the letter in a "for attention" pile in the hope that sometime I might come up with an idea. I did find some comment in an offbeat book on gardening by Warren G. Kenfield, *The Wild Gardener in the Wild Landscape*. The author thinks that lawn mowers are simply the modern version of a cow tethered by the house. The lawn, he says, is "a living fossil in a modern human zoo." In a footnote he explains, "I really like lawns. They have the pure clean simplicity of a freshly painted floor, or a bolt of monocolored cloth. I like them as I like sheathing evening gowns on other men's women, beautiful to look at, but horribly expensive to support."

Weeds (and lawns and gardens) seem to me to offer all sorts of possible projects for botanically minded students in city or suburban high schools. What plants are able to manage in the cracks of less-used sidewalks? What is the ecology of a vacant lot, and what weeds appear around an abandoned building? R. S. R. Fitter, in an excellent book, *London's Natural History* (in the Collins "New Naturalist" series; I think the book has not been published in this country, but it ought to be in the library of every metropolitan high school), lists 126 species of flowering plants and ferns found in bombed sites in London after the Second World War — avoiding sites which included gardens or parts of gardens "unless the species present prior to the bombing were known and could be excluded." I hope we won't have an opportunity to make comparable studies in this country, but there is plenty of chance for ecological observation of other kinds of destruction.

A surprising number of birds have taken to the urban and suburban environment, offering many possibilities for study. For the London area, Fitter lists 74 breeding species

that are resident through the year; 26 breeding species
that are found in summer only; 45 species that are winter
visitors; and 41 species that pass through in the course of
migration. John Kieran devotes quite a bit of space in
his book to the discussion of birds in New York, but does
not give any statistics. John Bull, in his *Birds of the New
York Area,* gives notes on 412 species, but his "New York
area" includes all of Long Island, southern counties of
New York State and northern counties of New Jersey,
thus including country that is far from strictly "urban"
though easy enough of access from the city.

I should think someone would have published an account
of bird life in Central Park, but I have not come across
any such. John Bull remarks that the park is "one of the
best places for migrant passerines and noteworthy for its
warblers; the best portion is the 'Ramble' between 72nd
and 81st streets." Of the "Ramble," John Kieran remarks
that "as many as twenty-nine species of warbler have been
observed on a single day in May."

Someone should write a book about city birds around
the world. It would make a nice ecological "project" and
a good excuse for travel. Do pigeons occur in all cities?
I asked my ornithological friend Robert Storer; he said
he couldn't remember seeing them in Madagascar, but he
wasn't sure. He was struck there by the absence of English
sparrows, now so common almost everywhere in the world.

In Honolulu the common street birds are mynahs, Chinese doves and English sparrows, getting along together
very nicely. The mynahs have a curious habit of "holding

court" — two birds fighting, surrounded by a ring of watchers seemingly intent on the outcome. The spectacle is said sometimes to stop traffic. For a while I saw no pigeons, but then I found a large flock that roosted under the eaves of the Bishop Museum, apparently going out to forage in the countryside during the day.

One summer in San Juan, Puerto Rico, the hotel where I stayed served breakfast on an outdoor terrace, and the charming little Puerto Rican honeycreepers invaded the tables to get tidbits from the guests. At night the grounds resounded with the bird-like calls of the coquí, that particularly vocal tree frog. A musician told me it was rumored that the governor sent out to collect coquís that could span a full octave (most coquís don't quite make it) for release in the Fortaleza, where he lives and entertains distinguished visitors.

Cities, undeniably, are quite different from rain forest or north woods; but this does not mean that they are devoid of natural history.

THE NATURAL HISTORY OF DISEASE

18

FOR SEVENTEEN YEARS I WORKED FOR THE International Health Division of the Rockefeller Foundation, chiefly concerned with the epidemiology of malaria in Europe and North Africa, and of yellow fever in South America. Epidemiology is ordinarily defined as the study of the incidence and spread of disease, which is another way of saying the environmental relationships of diseases — their ecology, or in my vocabulary their natural history. The subject continues to fascinate me, now not so much in terms of specific research as in relation to general aspects of the human ecosystem.

Disease is one of those words that everyone uses and understands — until asked for a definition. Dictionaries don't help much: disease is usually defined as a departure from a state of health, and health as the absence of disease, which is nicely circular. Clearly health and disease are polar words like hot and cold; but we can measure heat with a thermometer. What kind of measurement can we use for degrees of health? We have not found any so far. I like the proposal that death should be considered the absolute zero of health: as long as there is some life, there is some health. But we have difficulties with the other end of the scale, the "state of being hale or sound in body, mind or soul," as one dictionary puts it.

Body, mind and soul covers a lot of territory, which leads to the difficulty everyone has in making classifications of diseases. The infectious diseases, those caused by the invasion of the body by microorganisms, form a neat category — and one that generally receives the most attention. In the years after Pasteur's discoveries, there was a frantic search for a pathogen, an infectious agent, for every obvious disease. Failure in this brought to light the deficiency diseases — those due to the absence of some vitamin or mineral in the diet. Starvation, I suppose, could also be called a deficiency disease. Problems multiply when we become concerned with diseases due to hereditary defects, with mental disease, and with accidents. The well-being of the soul may be the province of theology or philosophy, but everyone has ideas and opinions.

Infectious diseases are complicated enough. From the point of view of natural history they can be classified into two large groups: the contagions, those that are "catching," passing directly from individual to individual; and those with some indirect method of transmission, such as passage through mosquitoes in the case of yellow fever or malaria.

Some of the diseases with indirect transmission have fantastically complicated life histories. The extreme is reached in the flukes (digenetic trematodes). There are some three thousand species of these, among them the pathogens causing the human disease schistosomiasis. All pass through a stage in snail hosts. There may be only one species of intermediate host, or there may be two. In the latter case both may be mollusks, one may be a snail and the other a crustacean, or the second intermediate host may be a larval insect, a fish, or an amphibian. These ultimately occur in various combinations with definitive vertebrate hosts, which may be fish, amphibia, birds or mammals.

I used to wonder why so many parasites had complicated life histories. It would seem simpler to be able to jump directly from host to host, like the measles virus in man; to be contagious. With indirect transmission the hazards of finding a suitable new host for each stage seem immense. It is hard to understand, for instance, how anyone becomes infected with malaria — yet millions of people do. The ordinary form of the parasite in the blood cells of man cannot infect mosquitoes. The infective forms of the parasite appear in the blood only occasionally and a man has to be bitten by an anopheline mosquito at this precise time if the mosquito is to become a vector. This mosquito must subsequently live for ten days to two weeks or more — until the parasites have become lodged in its salivary glands — before it can pass the disease on. The chances of a mosquito's surviving for two weeks in nature are slight. Then this mosquito has to bite a person susceptible to the disease — not a cow or a bird or some other kind of animal.

Furthermore, none of the anophelines has a really strong preference for biting people if some animal like a cow or goat is easily available, though a few, such as the African *Anopheles gambiae,* have habits which bring them into close association with people.

On the other hand, I can see that a parasite might not find it easy to get directly from one host to another of the same kind. Animals in nature are widely scattered; in the cases where large herds or flocks live together, there may be little contact between herds. There is a further difficulty in the case of self-limited infections, those in which disease is followed by immunity, as with measles and smallpox in man. There must always be a supply of fresh susceptible hosts available if the parasite is to persist, and two potential hosts would be safer than one. Also a parasite may be self-limited in one host and not in the other; with yellow fever, for instance, the virus can live in man for ten days or so, when the host either dies or becomes immune. But the virus can persist in a vector mosquito for as long as the mosquito lives. This may not be long, but yellow-fever vectors have been kept alive in the laboratory for more than thirty days. Perhaps the indirect transmission of disease, then, is a case in which ecological complexity promotes stability.

The directly transmitted diseases — the contagions — require a considerable number of possible hosts in frequent contact for survival; and this is especially true of the self-limited contagions like measles, mumps, smallpox and the various influenzas. These diseases get along fine in urban concentrations of people, where there are always newcomers and children to be exploited. But they are less easily maintained in scattered rural populations, particularly where there is no contact with cities. It is notorious that isolated groups of people will suffer an epidemic of the common cold after a ship has come in, but that the virus cannot maintain itself and there will be no more colds until some new infecting visitor arrives.

This has led me to suspect that the human contagions may be rather new diseases that developed when people first became crowded together in settlements after the beginnings of agriculture — after the Neolithic Revolution, 5,000 to 10,000 years ago. I have talked with several epidemiologists about this, and they agree that it is possible, though we can never have direct evidence. That an indirectly transmitted disease can become contagious is shown by bubonic plague, which normally is carried by fleas, but during an epidemic may take on a pneumonic form which can pass directly from person to person.

European diseases were new both to America and the Pacific islands when they were discovered. One can argue that it was smallpox, not Cortez, that conquered Mexico. The story is told in an interesting little book by E. W. and A. E. Stearn, *The Effect of Smallpox on the Destiny of the Amerindian.* "At the time of the departure of Narvaez from Cuba in order to join Cortez, smallpox was raging there severely. A pioneer vessel of the fleet brought the disease to Cozumel, whence it spread to the continent. . . . After desolating the coast regions, the disease crossed the plateau region and in the summer broke out around the lakes in passing to the land along the 'western sea.' For sixty days it raged with such virulence that the period of the raging of 'hueyzahuatl' or great pest, fixed itself as a central point in the chronology of the natives. In most districts half of the population died, towns became deserted, and those who recovered presented an appearance which horrified their neighbors. . . . In December, 1520, Cortez, on his way to Montezuma and the capital city of Mexico, stopped at Cholula, where he was asked to nominate new Indian chiefs to replace those dead from the smallpox."

I suspect that European diseases may have been primarily responsible for the almost complete elimination of the native population of Hispaniola and other West Indian islands. The history books blame the cruelty of the Spaniards, and there is no denying their heartlessness. But it seems unlikely that this alone could have caused the death of something like a million people in a few years. In the case of Polynesia and Micronesia, the drastic reduction of the population because of European diseases is well documented.

I find the notion amusing that the ships of Columbus and his successors brought malaria to the New World and took back syphilis in exchange. The ancientness of malaria in Europe is certain — the characteristic chills and fever are described in the Hippocratic writings and many subsequent accounts. The absence of the disease from America is less certain, since there is no direct proof, but the majority of students think that it came only with the Europeans.

The case for syphilis is also unsure. The disease did make a sudden and dramatic appearance in Europe at the end of the fifteenth century, but one can argue that it had been present all along and simply underwent a sudden increase in virulence. This has been known to happen with pathogens — witness the 1918 epidemic of influenza. Whether or not syphilis was brought back by the sailors of Columbus, its rapid spread across Europe must reflect pretty loose sexual habits in all ranks of people.

Historians have unduly neglected the role of disease in human events, as has been emphasized by Hans Zinsser in his fascinating book *Rats, Lice and History* — in which there is an amusing chapter on "The Unimportance of Generals." True, it is often difficult to be sure about the diagnosis of diseases of the past, but their importance is nevertheless clear.

It seems to me, for instance, that the relations between Europe and the rest of the world in modern times result at least in part from disease patterns. The easy conquest of the American civilizations may have been due as much to disease as to gunpowder, as I remarked. The failure of the Oriental civilizations to collapse on contact with Europeans may, then, be due to the fact that their populations had long shared European diseases. To be sure, Europe eventually conquered much of the Orient, but at the cost of a great deal of force and much trickery.

Tropical Africa, on the other hand, was long protected from European interference by its endemic diseases, to which Europeans were very susceptible. Africa is now considered to be the principal center of human evolution—and I suspect that it was also the center for the evolution of many human diseases. The parasites of malaria, for instance, may well have evolved right along with man in the African setting. Four different species of *Plasmodium* cause malaria in man, and these will not infect any other kind of vertebrate; various apes and monkeys also have their characteristic species of *Plasmodium,* and primates are the only mammals so infected (except for a recently discovered African rodent). The *Plasmodia* are associated with primates, birds and reptiles, which makes one think that the primate association is an ancient one.

Africa is also generally thought to be the original home of yellow fever, the disease being brought to America with the slave ships. The ships carried both the human hosts and the African vector mosquito, *Aëdes aegypti,* which bred in the water tanks on board. The mosquito became established in tropical American cities and towns, where it continued to breed mostly in man-made water containers. The virus also found suitable hosts in some of the American monkeys, and vectors among forest mosquitoes, leading to the establishment of "jungle yellow fever."

Africa remains the home of a considerable number of special diseases, with sleeping sickness (trypanosomiasis) the most spectacular. The vector of this is the tsetse fly (*Glossina*), which is found only in tropical Africa. Since these flies are the only vectors of the trypanosomes of sleeping sickness, the disease also remains limited to Africa—

which illustrates a disadvantage, from the point of view of the parasite, in needing two different hosts.

Tropical Africa gradually ceased to be a graveyard for Europeans during the twentieth century, with the growth in understanding of the epidemiology and treatment of tropical diseases. We still have much to learn about infectious diseases, but they are no longer on the list of major human problems. The control of disease, however, has led to the postponement of death, resulting in the present extremely rapid growth of human populations, especially in tropical countries. The disease problem has been replaced by the population problem, by the need to find some way of limiting human multiplication before we destroy our planet through sheer weight of numbers.

THE PSYCHOLOGICAL ZOO

19

STUDENTS OF ANIMAL BEHAVIOR MAKE A deal of fuss about the sin of anthropomorphism: the attribution of human feelings or understandings to other animals. But no one seems to be very bothered about zoomorphism: the ascription of animal traits to people — yet we do it all the time. Mostly this is not very flattering to the animals concerned, and they have no recourse for slander.

Reptiles are generally maligned: snake, lizard, toad. "Frog" is not meant to be complimentary when applied to a Frenchman. And whoever heard of a wealthy and respected fish? Birds and mammals don't always come off well either. Our treatment of the skunk bothers me: a charming animal, easily tamed, who happens to have an effective means of defense which he doesn't hesitate to use when provoked — but also a "contemptible, ill-mannered person," according to the dictionary.

"Look at that cool cat with the gorgeous chick!" Cats and chickens get particularly varied treatment in the psychological zoo. "Cat" gets two pages in the unabridged *Oxford English Dictionary*, without benefit of any of the modern slang uses. The word has a long history as a synonym for prostitute, but this was already obsolete at the time when the *OED* was compiled; clearly, though, the meaning has survived in the current term "cathouse." And then there is "catty," appropriate enough in its meaning of "stealthy" or "agile," but I don't quite see how it got the meaning of "given to malicious gossip," which seems to be the commonest usage nowadays. Tom cats, on the other hand, are understandable enough — whether people or felines — even if neither variety fits our professed ideals of moral virtue.

I have heard the opinion that the present use of "chick" may have come from *chic* rather than from poultry; but majority opinion holds it to be the diminutive form of "chicken." This seems entirely likely — "young and tender," another of the interminable list of vocabulary parallels between food and sex. There may also be overtones of "scatterbrained"; at least my limited contact with chicks would make this seem appropriate.

Then there is the scornful sense of "chicken." Poultry, to be sure, are not notable for bravery; but why should they be? Bravery strikes me as a much over-rated virtue. People might get into a lot less trouble if they were not so worried about acting like chickens. Chickens, of course, can be mean enough to one another. This, curiously, was not

formulated into a scientific theory until 1922 when a Norwegian, Schjelderup-Ebbe, described the peck order, or
dominance hierarchy, that he had observed in a flock of
chickens. Schjelderup-Ebbe jumped from his chickens to
the universe. "Despotism," he said, "is the basic idea of the
world, indissolubly bound up with all life and existence.
On it rests the meaning of the struggle for existence." Hens
peck one another; but bossing them all around is the strut-
ting cock. Rooster pride is but rarely dominated by the will
of some determined female — which gives "henpecked" its
pathetic force.

Hawks and doves have lately taken a prominent place in
the bird section of the psychological zoo. Doves, of course,
have been symbols of peace ever since that legendary bird
brought Noah tidings of the waning of the flood, while
fierce kings and nobles have long admired the hawk.

But there are problems with both words. For one thing,
neither has a clear-cut meaning. Hawks belong to the bird
family Accipitridae, which includes also eagles, Old World
vultures, kites and harriers. Whether a particular bird is
called a hawk or an eagle seems to be mostly a matter of
size, but I can see no reason for calling some hawks and
others kites. In England some of the birds we would call
hawks are called buzzards; our ancestors got mixed up when
they called the quite unrelated New World vultures "buzzards" — as so often has been the case with animal names.

Doves, along with pigeons, make up the family Colubri-
dae, with some 289 species widely distributed around the
world. Again, I can find no basis for calling some birds

"dove" and others "pigeon" except historical accident. In one dictionary the definition of "dove" is simply "pigeon." The domestic pigeon is descended from the common rock dove of Europe and Asia; and with English logic, we still keep pigeons in dovecots.

What about the human hawks and doves? It seems as though they could just as readily be called buzzards and pigeons — which puts a quite different light on their characters, and which also shows how far we depend on the connotations of words rather than on the traits of the animals themselves. Konrad Lorenz, in his delightful book on animal behavior, *King Solomon's Ring*, maintains that doves really have quite nasty characters. They manage to get along with one another fairly well in the wild because when one bird attacks another the loser can escape by flying. But if a fight starts between two caged birds, there is no end until one or the other is killed — there is no forgiveness or charity among doves. This, as Lorenz points out, makes them an inappropriate symbol for peace.

He also notes that most predatory animals have behavioral inhibitions which prevent them from inflicting damage on one another — the evolution of powerful claws, teeth and beaks has been accompanied by the evolution of controlling behavior with regard to other members of the same species. As birds of prey, then, hawks should be peaceful animals. I haven't, in fact, come across any stories of hawks being mean to other hawks of the same kind, though the rest of the animal kingdom is fair game. Hawks range in size from species no bigger than doves to the giant monkey-eating species of the tropics, and almost everything serves as food for some species or other: insects, fish, reptiles, mammals, other kinds of birds are all possible hawk prey. There is even a species in the American tropics, known as the Everglade kite in Florida, that feeds on snails — they hold the snails until they crawl partway out of their shells, and then spear them.

Many kinds of hawks have been observed to feed on carrion. This always seems to upset hawk-lovers, though I don't see why, since the Old World vultures are close relatives. Even the gigantic and powerful griffon vulture never kills food — will not in fact touch an animal that shows signs of life. As a model for human behavior, the griffon vulture appears to me more admirable than most hawks — the human hawks, of whatever nationality, could certainly do with a little such restraint.

Hawks are also frequently given to stealing. One of the most notorious thieves is that hawk-relative, the bald eagle — our national emblem. This eagle lives largely on fish, which it can catch for itself; but it also gets meal by harassing that expert fisherman the osprey, forcing it to drop its catch. Benjamin Franklin argued that the wild turkey would be a more suitable emblem than the eagle. I suppose if his idea had prevailed Thanksgiving might have taken on the aspects of a ritual totemic feast. Humans are not often called turkeys in my experience, but such usage as does occur is not flattering to the people or the birds. I find, in Wentworth and Flexner's *Dictionary of American Slang,* meaning 9, "An ineffective, incompetent, objectionable or disliked person." The meaning, said to be current, is illustrated by a quotation about collectors of internal revenue.

I am puzzled by how mean we are to dogs — and bitches — in the psychological zoo. I am reminded of a remark by Mouse in Walt Kelley's *G. O. Fizzickle Pogo:* "One thing is sure! If dogs are man's best friend, he better keep 'em . . . It's better than nothing." Why isn't it all right to call a man a dog, since they are our closest companions among the animals? Bitches in heat can certainly be sexually promiscuous, which is "bad" in the tradition of Western society; but I have never noticed anything particularly bitchy about canine females at other times. The human bitch is something else again.

In many cultures dogs serve as scavengers; and they certainly lead a miserable-looking existence, kicked by every passing human, half-starved and "wolfing" every possible bit of food they can find. Maybe our usage is a hangover from this sort of attitude in the Middle Ages. Of course even our civilized dogs sometimes show habits that distress their owners: rolling in carrion, raiding garbage, identifying each other by the smell of anal glands. But this hardly explains why "dog" should be such a powerful insult.

Support for the scavenger theory comes from a similar treatment of the words "pig," "swine" and "hog," since these animals also frequently carry out garbage and sewage services in primitive villages. Many people who have been closely associated with swine maintain that they are really intelligent animals, capable of becoming affectionate pets.

The Jewish taboo on pork, continued by Islam, is generally thought to be based on reaction to a widespread
heathenish pig cult in the early Mediterranean, as I mentioned in the chapter on food habits. On the other hand,
pigs are generally liked by villagers and scorned by no-
madic pastoral peoples, so that their prohibition may result
from pastoral influence.

Rats have at least as bad a reputation among people as
do pigs. According to Lorenz, the rat reputation is justified
by their fighting habits; but I understand that one of the
valid criticisms of his book *On Aggression* is that he makes
too strong a case out of the conflict behavior of rats. Certainly, however, they are unloved by most humans. A friend
once asked me about the South American capybaras. I explained that they looked like pigs, but were really a kind
of rat. "But that's me!" was his exclamation. I suppose
everyone feels that way at times, but the capybara syndrome
hasn't got into our language.

We do have many other stereotypes about our domesticated animals: jackass, donkey; mulish, cow-like, bullish.
There are also quite a few old goats about, some perfect
lambs, and some people who feel sheepish. Black sheep, as
the oddballs, probably got their reputation simply from being different. Horses come out fairly well (except for their
rear end), though serious-minded people may disapprove
of horseplay.

I can think of only one case where an animal got its name
from human behavior, rather than vice versa: "sloth" has
a long history in English as a term for human indolence

or laziness. This, when the animal was discovered, seemed an apt label for the dim-witted, deliberate mammal of the South American trees.

But zoomorphisms are innumerable: sometimes appropriate, perhaps more often not. Think of the connotations of bat, fox, badger, beaver, mouse, lion, monkey. And I have completely ignored insects: wasps, lice, worms, bees and irresponsible butterflies. They make up a considerable zoological garden —fascinating, even though the inhabitants have little relation with reality.

BLACK, WHITE AND COLORED

20

WE HAVE, IN THE UNITED STATES, BE-
come burdened with a whole complex of attitudes and beliefs about race that form a frighteningly explosive mixture.
The problems are clearly social rather than biological, aris-
ing out of developments in the cultural history of Western
civilization as a whole, and of the United States in particular. The solutions will also necessarily involve culture
change. Yet race — geographical variation within an animal
species — is a biological phenomenon, which may give me
some excuse for contributing to the mass of verbiage that
has been generated in the discussion of racial problems.

Our vocabulary annoys me. I find "white" a particularly
silly term for peoples of European and Near Eastern origin.
Albinos, which may turn up almost anywhere, might be
called white; but with that exception I can't see how
the word could apply to any human skin. "Of the color of
snow or milk," the dictionary says of white. My efforts to

imagine a human complexion blending into a snowbank are unavailing. Ermine may be white, but not people. Europeans, when they stay out of the sun, tend to be lighter than most other people; but the best term for this would seem to be "paleface," allegedly used by the American Indians.

There are all sorts of troubles with connotations when we use "white" and "black." One of the subsidiary meanings of "white" is "morally or spiritually pure or stainless"; and *The Oxford English Dictionary* has another subsidiary meaning (7b): "free from malignity or evil intent; beneficent, innocent, harmless, esp. as opposed to something characterized as *black*." We have, for instance, the difference between white magic and black. We of European descent might like to think of ourselves as white in this sense of being innocent and beneficent; but such a belief is hardly held up by history.

The problem was already bothering me back in 1952 when I wrote the chapter on "The Varieties of Tropical Man" in *Where Winter Never Comes*. I suggested there that we might be better off if we used words based on Greek: for white skin, *leucoderm;* for black, *melanoderm;* for yellow, *xanthoderm;* for red, *erythroderm*. It would seem to me much more difficult to get upset about leucoderms versus melanoderms than about white versus black.

There isn't, of course, any chance of influencing change in vocabulary, but it is still fun to play with the idea. White superiority, in the Greek-based vocabulary, would become "leucodermosis," which has an appropriately diseased sound. Black Power might comparably become "melanodermosis."

I know some Negroes who suffer from acute forms of melanodermosis. This is perfectly understandable, but hardly helpful in solving the problems of coexistence. It is a more reasonable disease than leucodermosis — one wonders why it has not affected everyone labeled "Negro" — but it still seems unhealthy. In its acute form it becomes leucophobia, a hatred for all palefaces.

The Greek terms would give a new perspective on segregation. Restaurants and bars could put up signs saying "Only Leucoderms Will Be Served," which would look appropriately ridiculous. And it might be possible to work out a quarantine for real-estate agents infected with melanophobia. At least such a label would seem apt for this particular kind of social disease.

One of the problems of racial names stems from the accident by which the aboriginal Americans came to be called Indians. This leaves us with the awkward necessity of always using an adjective to show whether American or Indian Indians are meant. One solution has been to call the Americans "Amerinds," but this sounds to me more like a label for a variety of fruit than for a variety of people. Erythroderm doesn't help much in this case, since the need is not so much for ridicule as for a workaday word.

The American Anthropological Association, in the course of its 1967 meetings, held a special symposium on "War." In connection with this Sol Tax attempted to assess the relative popularity of the various wars in which the United States has been involved. I was surprised to learn that the Indian wars of our past had the greatest popular support of all. On reflection, though, this is understandable. The Indians were generally considered inferior and we wanted their lands — so we took them. I have been told that the United States has broken more treaties than any other modern nation because of the habitual failure to honor agreements made with the Indians.

Our hatred of the Indians has subsided since we have them out of the way, nicely herded into reservations on land for which we have little use. But the problems of leucoderm-erythroderm remain, with no likely solution in sight. We have, to a varying but large extent, undermined the values of the Indian cultures without replacing them with our own — creating a situation that looks unsatisfactory to almost everyone. Must the Indians be Westernized, absorbed into our society? Cultural diversity appeals to me as a "good thing" in itself; but not if it has to be maintained artificially on fenced reservations, dealing with vanishing cultures as we deal with vanishing wildlife.

The situation of the erythroderms in the United States is thus very different from that of the melanoderms. The Africans were torn out of their native cultures and thrust into ours. Over the generations they have acquired our values; they are Americans, which makes the caste discrimination all the more painful and senseless. James Baldwin has given a sensitive description of his personal discovery of his Americanism in *Notes of a Native Son,* and his experience is surely far from unique. Here, incidentally, we have the case of an extremely good writer who happens to have the wrong skin color.

Wrong? It is odd that a beautiful skin should be a handicap; and I, at least, find the darker human skins more attractive than the pale ones. This must be generally true if one can judge by the amount of time paleface people spend in trying to darken their skins. Suntan lotions, sunlamps and beaches for sunbathing form a considerable industry. This leucoderm preoccupation with getting dark must look ridiculous to a melanoderm; it certainly makes melanophobia seem odd.

There is, of course, no such thing as a "race" in any objective sense. Some students recognize three or four races, others thirty or more, but in no case is it possible to draw sharp lines. Ashley Montagu and a few other anthropologists think it would be helpful if we abandoned the word "race" altogether and, since human differences are undeniable, wrote about "ethnic groups." I can't see that this would help much. Anyway, they have about as much chance of changing vocabulary as I have of persuading people to use "leucoderm" instead of "white." The real need in many of these cases is not so much to substitute words as it is to desensitize the words we already have.

The differences among groups of people that we classify as racial traits are puzzling. They include skin color, hair form and distribution, facial features and body build, as well as differences in blood chemistry and presumably in other aspects of internal anatomy and physiology. For most of these traits I cannot see any adaptive value, though many students of the subject would disagree with me. Dark skin color, for instance, at first appears to be an adaptation to warm climates. But in the infrared parts of the spectrum involved in heat transfer, all human skin acts as a "black body," absorbing and radiating heat with equal efficiency. All efforts to show racial differences in heat toleration have failed. (Relevant studies have been summarized in an article by H. F. Blum entitled "Does the Melanin Pigment of Human Skin Have Adaptive Value?" in the issue of the *Quarterly Review of Biology* for January 1961.) Some of the proposed adaptive explanations seem to verge on the absurd: that the epicanthic fold of the Mongolian eye is a protection against the glare of snow fields; or that the same Mongolians have little facial hair because ice crystals, forming in a beard, would be inconvenient.

But it is difficult to explain many human features, whether they characterize particular races or the species as a whole. Desmond Morris, in *The Naked Ape,* has looked at the possible evolutionary background of many human peculiarities; and his ideas, whether valid or not, should at least stimulate discussion. He reviews, for instance, the various explanations of our lack of body fur: that it makes it easier to catch lice and fleas; that primitive man was a messy feeder and could not keep fur clean; that the loss of fur was a consequence of the acquisition of fire; that the fur was lost during an aquatic stage in human evolution. He seems himself to favor the idea that the naked body would have a cooling advantage in the quick spurts of running by primitive hunters.

Leucoderms don't come out very well if we compare different races in biological terms. The trait of hairlessness, for instance: we have more body hair than any other human type, which would make us backward in comparison with the more hairless melanoderms and xanthoderms. The lips form another human peculiarity, the inside lining of the mouth coming outside (Morris thinks this serves as a sexual signal). The melanoderms would win here too, with their thicker lips. In general, the melanoderms seem to be the most advanced of racial varieties — and Africa appears to be the center of human evolution — which gives no help to people suffering from leucodermosis.

But generalization of this sort is dangerous. I found a book by the distinguished biochemist Roger Williams, entitled *You Are Extraordinary*, particularly interesting in this respect. Williams is attacking the concept of the "normal" or "average" man, which could equally well apply to the average for any race. We all know that individuals look different and have distinctive fingerprints; if we stop to think, we realize that each has a different smell — as every bloodhound knows. Our insides differ greatly: stomachs come in all sorts of shapes and sizes; the heart is even more variable than the stomach; sense organs differ in acuity from person to person, and so on through all aspects of our anatomy and physiology.

We have to be careful then in generalizing about man or about different races. It isn't the race that counts, but the individual; and each individual is different. I particularly like an analogy made by Williams: "Social science built on the average man would be like United States geography built upon the concept of the 'average state': It has an area of 72,000 square miles and a population of over 3.5 million. It has about 1,200 square miles of fresh water lakes and 37 square miles of salt lake. Its highest mountains are about 6,000 feet high. About 5,000 square miles of it lie in the Arctic regions, where the ground is frozen the year round (permafrost). It has a shoreline of about 150 miles. The average state produces yearly about 1/2 million barrels of oil; 300,000 tons of coal; 50,000 pounds of copper; 10 million bushels of wheat; 3 million pounds of tobacco; 1 million bales of cotton; about 150,000 tons of citrus fruit and 9,000 tons of pineapples."

No one fits the average. We are not black, white or colored. We are individuals, you and me.

VALUES OF DIVERSITY

21

$\mathbf{S}$ OME PEOPLE EAT WITH A KNIFE AND FORK, others with chopsticks, and still others use their fingers. Among the knife-and-fork people, the British think Americans are funny because of the way they keep shifting the fork from left to right hand; Americans, on the other hand, may be fascinated by the British skill in stashing peas in the mashed potatoes on the back of the fork — held always in the left hand. To each of us, of course, our way of doing things is the right way. This would not matter much if it were not for the complications of the missionary syndrome, which leads us to try to persuade other people to abandon their ways and take up ours.

The etiquette of eating is trivial, except maybe at diplomatic dinners, where I suppose that an ambassador, picking up the wrong fork, might seriously compromise the international standing of his country. But our attitudes toward food — kinds and ways of eating it — illustrate an intolerance that has deeper and far more serious aspects. This is what led me to start a book entitled *Gluttons and Libertines* with the idea of ridiculing our attitudes toward sex by finding parallels in the less highly charged attitudes toward food. I soon found myself going beyond food and sex and writing a sort of general plea for the tolerance of diversity.

There are, of course, many kinds of diversity. In the world of nature we have the possibility of diversity in the gene pool of a given species of organism; diversity in kinds of plants and animals in a biological community; diversity in kinds of communities, from desert to rain forest or from ocean depths to coral reef.

Diversity in the gene pool of a species provides the raw material for evolution, makes possible adaptation to changing environments, allows for flexibility. Diversity in the biological community, on the other hand, makes for stability and continuity. This can be seen in the contrast between the relatively simple communities of the far north and the complex aggregations of animals and plants that make up a tropical rain forest or a coral reef. The animal populations in the far north fluctuate greatly, though more or less regularly, from year to year, as is nicely shown by the fur records of the Hudson's Bay Company over a period of a hundred years. In the case of snowshoe hares and lynx, an increase in the number of hares is followed by an increase in the predatory lynx, until the hare population is reduced to scarcity again — leading in turn to a decline in the numbers of lynx. This results in a fairly regular series of cyclic fluctuations at about ten-year intervals. Such cyclic fluctuations are unknown in the rain forest, where the complexity of prey-predator relations makes for flexibility and results in a relatively steady state for all populations. But the various arguments for maintaining diversity in biological systems are well summarized by that great British ecologist, Charles Elton, in a chapter on "The Conservation of Variety" in a book published in 1958, *The Ecology of Invasions.*

The diversity in biological communities has enabled life to take advantage of almost all of the varied conditions on our planetary surface — the chief exceptions being ice caps and extreme deserts. What variety there is! Somehow we must keep these varied landscapes from being entirely swamped by human alterations, so that future generations can in some degree share experience with the wilderness.

There is need for diversity among people, too, whether looked at as individuals, as communities or as large societies. We try to recognize the need of the individual in our educational system, attempting to give everyone, whatever his future specialty, some background in the arts, the sciences and the humanities; some experience with differing points of view. The fact that we do not succeed very well is no reflection on the soundness of the idea. In another way, the concept of "vacation" expresses our felt need for refreshing change. The cult of hobbies, again, is manifestation of diversity in the activities of individuals; and as work becomes more monotonous, more specialized, the need for escape with vacation or hobby becomes greater.

Beyond this, there is the matter of diversity of roles

within a society — and diversity of cultures among societies. Contemporary Western civilization must have a greater variety of possible roles than any previous culture, a consequence of our increasing specialization. Yet there is still a great and valid outcry against the pressures for conformity. I think this is because we have many possible occupations, but few permissible styles of life. The monotony shows in the rows of little boxes in the suburbs, in the standardized education, in the multiplying chain stores and shopping centers, in the routine of the assembly line. And monotony, meaninglessness and frustration are compounded in our ghettos.

The West, in the last few hundred years, has had a bull-dozing effect on other cultures. Our power to enforce our ideas is declining, but it still has considerable momentum. I remember reading somewhere that Indonesia, influenced by Western ideas of modesty, had required the dancing girls of Bali to cover their breasts. The Japanese are said to be somewhat worried about Western attitudes toward their abortion laws. And it seems to me particularly odd to see Japanese, Malays, Hindus, Nigerians dressed up in our silly Western clothing. There is a growing movement to retain indigenous dress, but it is still not quite respectable in diplomatic circles. I sometimes suspect that the chief trouble with Fidel Castro is his beard and windbreaker. It probably ought to be his interminable speeches — but you can hardly carry out diplomatic negotiations with a man wearing a windbreaker.

The opposite of diversity is uniformity. An interesting

word — uniform. Standardized dress serves to depersonalize the soldier, the policeman, the waiter or bellboy. The effect is to convert individuals into abstractions, symbols of some occupation or hierarchical rank, drab units in a "brave new world."

In this connection I find the nonconforming antics of our young fascinating, and there is plenty of chance for observation in a university environment. They are obviously rebelling against the adult world that they are entering — I can't blame them when I look at the mess we have made of things — and they flaunt the inner rebellion with an outer show of diversity in dress. It at least succeeds in upsetting the police, the school authorities and probably the parents, a reaction that I fail to understand except in terms of our unease about anything different. The "beats" of a few years ago seemed pretty uniform — conforming to the standards of the group, however different these might be from the standards of the larger society. But I see no such uniformity in the youth of today. The only uniformity is the effort to be different, to be individuals.

The boys may have long hair or short, sideburns, beards, mustaches, goatees; they may go barefooted or wear boots or (perhaps most commonly) dirty sneakers. Their trousers may be tight or loose, levis or corduroys, or shorts made by attacking the trousers with a pair of scissors; they may wear an earring and/or a variety of kinds of ornaments hung around the neck. They sometimes manage to look quite dirty, but I suspect most of them bathe often enough. What is all the fuss about?

Some of the boys, with their neatly trimmed and combed long hair, look as though they might have stepped out of some castle in the Middle Ages; more, I am afraid, look like seventeenth-century pirates; and the beards are often reminiscent of the fashions of the last century, as sometimes are the "mod" clothes.

A large proportion of the girls have taken to wearing masculine clothing. This is understandable in practical terms — at least they get pockets. I sometimes wonder, though, at the amount of trouble they must take to look so disheveled; anyway the effect seems contrived rather than accidental.

The consequence of these boy-girl tendencies in dress is to minimize the differences between the sexes, which are exaggerated by our traditional clothing. I am reminded of Geoffrey Gorer's observation, quoted in an earlier chapter, that nonaggressive human societies "make very little distinction between the ideal characters of men and women." I really think our young are nonaggressive; the fierce posturings are made by people of my generation, in no immediate danger of landing on the firing line.

An editor of the *Toledo Blade* called me up a while ago to ask for my reaction to an ordinance enacted by the Toledo City Council making it illegal for "any homosexual, lesbian or perverted person" to appear in public in the dress of the opposite sex. We agreed that it was a silly ordinance in a world where Daddy's shirts and trousers were no longer safe from pilfering daughters. I have made no Kinsey-like study of the matter, but I have the impression that there is no homosexual element in the clothing habits of our young. The opposite seems more likely: that they reflect an easy and casual attitude toward heterosexual relations which horrifies the older generation, who after all had little chance for comparable experience. Besides, what is wrong with diversity in sexual behavior? Our attitude in this, the anthropologists would remind us, is purely cultural — as it is in most matters.

How do we distinguish right from wrong in the puzzling, relative world in which we live? I like the answer given by Philip Wylie — perhaps best known for *Generation of Vipers* — in a more recent book entitled *The Magic Animal*. It is a shrill, almost paranoid book, which sometimes sounds as though only the author clearly understands what a mess we are making of things. The standard of ethics, the "biological imperative," that he proposes would be to judge actions in terms of the needs of posterity. Not in terms of our own family, or of future Americans or Japanese, but in terms of "all the children of mankind." "To evaluate a culture properly," he writes, "one must balance its gains and deficits in relation to the future generations of all human beings."

This would leave most of our daily behavior ethically neutral, whether concerned with work or play, food or sex (unless unduly contributing to the population problem); but it would condemn our wanton exploitation of resources, our damage to the environment of this "spaceship earth" in which those future generations will have to live. What has this got to do with diversity? It leaves a wide range of tolerance of individual and cultural behavior that is not destructive; and it implies a command to maintain the diversity of the biosphere so that our children too can enjoy clear trout streams, giant redwoods, deep canyons and open spaces.

I think there is a corollary: that we should tolerate diversity in behavior to the extent that it does not damage the continuity of society. Antisocial activities should be classified as "crimes." But who is to decide what is anti-social, and how can it be decided? Murder, genocide and war seem to me clearly evil: but all can be, and have been justified in terms of the "good" of continuing society. And I am sure there are people in our country who regard boys wearing earrings as a sign of the collapse of all our treasured values, a mark of social disintegration.

The answer probably lies in "common sense." But whose, yours or mine? We can't all think alike — that would be uniformity instead of diversity. So let's argue — but let's not kill one another in the process.

MARSTON BATES

At a ceremony in 1967, when Marston Bates received the Charles P. Daly Medal of the American Geographical Society of New York, the citation read in part: "Marston Bates wears an almost bewildering variety of scholarly hats, and all of them become him. He is at one and the same time biologist, zoologist, medical ecologist, naturalist, humanist, and unquestionably, also, geographer manqué...

"During his many years of association with the International Health Division of the Rockefeller Foundation and, more recently, as professor of zoology at the University of Michigan, Dr. Bates has had the opportunity to work and observe in different parts of the world, but especially in Latin America and the South Pacific. We are the richer for his experience in these areas, since he is one of the too few scientists with a gift for clear and literate exposition. Whether he is writing about the origin and development of a coral atoll, the life history of a mosquito, the ambience of a tropical rain forest, or the problems of population pressure, he is able always to explain complex processes in terms that can be readily understood. Moreover, his style displays a philosophic bent, an acuity of perception, and a spark of humor that together make for delightful reading."

Bibliography

Anderson, A. W., *How We Got Our Flowers*. New York, Dover Publications, Inc., 1966. Reprint of 1951 publication by Ernest Benn, Ltd.

Ardrey, Robert, *The Territorial Imperative*. New York, Atheneum Publishers, 1966.

Bailey, L. H., "The Indigen and Cultigen." *Science,* Vol. 47, 1918, pp. 306-308.

——, *Hortus Second. A Concise Dictionary of Gardening, General Horticulture and Cultivated Plants in North America*. New York, The Macmillan Company, 1941.

Barbour, Thomas, *Naturalist at Large*. Boston, Little, Brown and Company, 1943.

Bates, Marston, *The Nature of Natural History*. New York, Charles Scribner's Sons, 1950.

——, *Where Winter Never Comes*. New York, Charles Scribner's Sons, 1952.

——, *Man in Nature,* 2nd ed. Englewood Cliffs, Prentice-Hall, Inc., 1964.

——, *Gluttons and Libertines: Human Problems of Being Natural*. New York, Random House, 1967.

Bates, Marston, and Abbott, Donald P., *Coral Island: Portrait of an Atoll*. New York, Charles Scribner's Sons, 1958.

Bates, Nancy Bell, *East of the Andes and West of Nowhere*. New York, Charles Scribner's Sons, 1947.

Blum, H. F., "Does the Melanin Pigment of Human Skin Have Adaptive Value?" *Quarterly Review of Biology,* Vol. 36, 1961, pp. 50-63.

Brown, John Pairman, *The Displaced Person's Almanac*. Boston, Beacon Press, 1962.

Bull, John L., *Birds of the New York Area*. New York, Harper & Row, 1964.

Calhoun, J. B., "Population Density and Social Pathology." *Scientific American,* Vol. 206, No. 2, 1962, pp. 139-148.

Carson, Rachel, *The Silent Spring*. Boston, Houghton Mifflin Company, 1962.

Cathey, H. M., and Downs, R. J., "Regulating the Flowering of Bromeliads." Three-page reprint from *The Exchange,* n.d. Articles on the flowering of bromeliads can also be found in *The Bromeliad Society Bulletin,* May/June, 1966 and May/June, 1968.

Charter, S P R, *Man on Earth: A Preliminary Evaluation of the Ecology of Man*. Sausalito, Contact Editions, 1962.

Clough, G. C., "Lemmings and Population Problems." *American Scientist,* Vol. 53, 1965, pp. 199-212.

Cutright, Paul Russell, *Lewis and Clark: Pioneering Naturalists*. Urbana, University of Illinois Press, 1969.

Dart, Raymond A., and Craig, Dennis, *Adventures with the Missing Link*. New York, Harper & Row, 1959.

Davis, David E., "The Characteristics of Rat Populations." *Quarterly Review of Biology*, Vol. 28, 1953, pp. 373-401.

Dembeck, Hermann, *Animals and Men*. New York, Natural History Press, 1965.

De Vore, Irven, ed., *Primate Behavior: Field Studies of Monkeys and Apes*. New York, Holt, Rinehart & Winston, 1965.

Durrell, Gerald, *Menagerie Manor*. New York, The Viking Press, Inc., 1964.

Edelson, Edward, and Warshofsky, Fred, *Poisons in the Air*. New York, Pocket Books, 1966.

Ehrlich, Paul, *The Population Bomb*. New York, Ballantine Books, Inc., 1968.

Elton, Charles, *Voles, Mice and Lemmings: Problems in Population Dynamics*. Oxford, Clarendon Press, 1942.

——, *The Ecology of Invasions*. New York, John Wiley & Sons, Inc., 1958.

Evans, Howard E., *Life on a Little Known Planet*. New York, E. P. Dutton & Co., Inc., 1968. The article on cockroaches referred to in Chapter IV is now a chapter in this book.

Farb, Peter, and the Editors of *Life, Ecology*. New York, Time-Life Books, 1963.

Fitter, R. S. R., *London's Natural History*. London, William Collins Sons & Co. Ltd., 1946.

Gorer, Geoffrey, "Man Has No 'Killer' Instinct." *New York Times Magazine* (November 27, 1966). Reprinted in Ashley Montagu, ed., *Man and Aggression*.

Grant, Karen A. and Verne, *Hummingbirds and Their Flowers*. New York, Columbia University Press, 1968.

Greenewalt, Crawford H., *Hummingbirds*. New York, Doubleday & Company, Inc., 1960.

Hediger, Heini, *Wild Animals in Captivity*. New York, Dover Publications, Inc., 1964.

Herber, Lewis, *Crisis in Our Cities*. Englewood Cliffs, Prentice-Hall Inc., 1965.

Howard, H. E., *Territory in Bird Life*. London, John Murray, 1920.

Howard, L. O., and Marlatt, C. L., *The Principal Household Insects of the United States*. 1896.

Jacobs, Jane, *The Death and Life of Great American Cities*. New York, Random House, 1961.

Kenfield, Warren G., *The Wild Gardener in the Wild Landscape*. New York, Hafner Publishing Co., Inc., 1966.

Keyfitz, Nathan, "Population Density and the Style of Social Life." *BioScience*, Vol. 16, 1966, pp. 868-873.

Kieran, John, *A Natural History of New York City.* Boston, Houghton Mifflin Company, 1959.

Kramer, Jack, *Bromeliads: The Colorful House Plants.* Princeton, Van Nostrand Reinhold Company, 1965.

Krutch, Joseph Wood, *The Great Chain of Life.* Boston, Houghton Mifflin Company, 1957.

Laessle, Albert M., "A Microlimnological Study of Jamaican Bromeliads." *Ecology,* Vol. 42, 1961, pp. 499-517.

Laycock, George, *The Alien Animals.* New York, Natural History Press, 1966.

Lorenz, Konrad, *King Solomon's Ring.* New York, Thomas Y. Crowell Company, 1952.

——, *On Aggression.* New York, Harcourt, Brace & World, Inc., 1966.

Lutz, Frank, *A Lot of Insects: Entomology in a Suburban Garden.* New York, G. P. Putnam's Sons, 1941.

Marsh, George Perkins, *Man and Nature,* David Lowenthal, ed. Cambridge, Harvard University Press, 1965. Based on the first edition, published in 1865 by Charles Scribner's Sons.

Marx, Wesley, *The Frail Ocean.* New York, Coward-McCann, Inc., 1967.

Montagu, M. F. Ashley, ed., *Man and Aggression.* New York, Oxford University Press, 1968.

Morris, Desmond, *The Naked Ape.* New York, McGraw-Hill Book Company, 1968.

Morris, Ramona and Desmond, *Men and Snakes.* New York, McGraw-Hill Book Company, 1965.

Mumford, Lewis, *The Myth of the Machine: Technics and Human Development.* New York, Harcourt, Brace & World, Inc., 1967.

Munro, George C., *Birds of Hawaii.* Rutland, Charles E. Tuttle Co., Inc., 1960.

Nice, Margaret, "The Role of Territory in Bird Life." *American Midland Naturalist,* Vol. 26, 1941, pp. 441-487.

Pitelka, F. A., "Territoriality and Related Problems in North American Hummingbirds." *The Condor,* Vol. 44, 1942, pp. 189-204.

Report of the National Advisory Commission on Civil Disorders. Otto Kerner, chairman, New York, E. P. Dutton & Co., Inc., 1968.

Rick, Charles M., and Bowman, Robert I., "Galápagos Tomatoes and Tortoises." *Evolution,* Vol. 15, 1961, pp. 407-417.

Rublowsky, John, *Nature in the City.* New York, Basic Books, Inc., 1967.

Sauer, C. O., *Agricultural Origins and Dispersals.* New York, American Geographical Society, 1952.

Schaller, George B., *The Mountain Gorilla: Ecology and Behavior.* Chicago, University of Chicago Press, 1963.

——, *The Year of the Gorilla.* Chicago, University of Chicago Press, 1964.

Scheithauer, Walter, *Hummingbirds.* New York, Thomas Y. Crowell Company, 1967.

Schjelderup-Ebbe, Thorleif, "Beiträge zur Sozial-psychologie des Haus-huhns." *Zeitschrift für Psychologie,* Vol. 88, 1922, pp. 225-252.

Schwanitz, Franz, *The Origin of Cultivated Plants.* Cambridge, Harvard University Press, 1966.

Simoons, Frederick J., *Eat Not This Flesh.* Madison, University of Wisconsin Press, 1961.

Simpson, George Gaylord, *Biology and Man.* New York, Harcourt, Brace & World, Inc., 1969. The *American Scholar* article referred to in Chapter XVI forms a chapter in this book.

Skutch, Alexander F., *Life Histories of Central American Birds.* Berkeley, Cooper Ornithological Society, Pacific Coast Avifauna No. 31, 1954.

Smith, Stuart, and Hosking, Eric, *Birds Fighting.* London, Faber and Faber, 1955.

Srole, Leo, and others, *Mental Health in the Metropolis,* Vol. 1. New York, McGraw-Hill Book Company, 1962.

Stearn, E. W. and A. E., *The Effect of Smallpox on the Destiny of the Amerindian.* Boston, Humphries, Inc., 1945.

Stewart, George Rippey, *Not so Rich as You Think.* Boston, Houghton Mifflin, Inc., 1968.

Storr, Anthony, *Human Aggression.* New York, Atheneum Publishers, 1968.

Tax, Sol, "War and the Draft." *Natural History,* Vol. 76, No. 10 (December, 1967), pp. 54-58.

Thompson, G. M., *The Naturalization of Animals and Plants in New Zealand.* Cambridge, Cambridge University Press, 1922.

Uvarov, B. P., *Locusts and Grasshoppers.* London, Imperial Bureau of Entomology, 1928.

Wentworth, Harold, and Flexner, S. B., *Dictionary of American Slang.* New York, Thomas Y. Crowell Company, 1960.

White, Lynn, Jr., "The Historical Roots of our Ecologic Crisis." *Science,* Vol. 155, 1967, pp. 1203-1207.

Williams, Roger J., *You Are Extraordinary.* New York, Random House, Inc., 1967.

Wylie, Philip, *The Magic Animal.* New York, Doubleday & Company, Inc., 1968.

Zinsser, Hans, *Rats, Lice and History.* Boston, Little, Brown & Company, 1935.

INDEX

Spinach 32, 73
Stearn, E. W. and A. E. 176-177
Stewart, George R. 112-119
Storer, Robert 170
Storr, Anthony 138
sunbirds 27

tanagers 17, 20, 27
Tax, Sol 191
territory 55, 143
  birds 32-33, 143-145
  herps 54-56
  howler monkeys 146
  humans 135-137, 146
Thompson, G. M. 152
Thraupidae 27
Tillandsia usneoides 65
Tinbergen, Niko 23, 140
Tinkle, Donald 49
titmice 28, 70-71
Trochilidae 27
Trypetidae 121
turtles 41, 54-55

Udall, Stewart 87
Uta palmeri 49
Uvarov, B. P. 122

Walker, Joseph P. 168
Warshofsky, Fred 167
weaverbirds 16
weeds 79, 149, 168-169
Westernization 178, 192, 200
White, Lynn, Jr. 90-91, 93
white-eyes 27-28
Williams, Roger 195-196
Wilson, Marjorie Kerr 141
Wylie, Philip 203

yellow fever 172-173, 179
  jungle yellow fever 58, 179

Zinsser, Hans 178
zoomorphisms 181-188
zoos 16, 19, 22, 74-75, 188
Zosteropidae
  Zosterops borbonica 27

214